Urbit Systems Technical Journal

Vol. 1, No. 2, 2024 : The Journal of Solid-State Computing

Urbit Systems Technical Journal

Welcome to the second issue of the *Urbit Systems Technical Journal: The Journal of Solid-State Computing*. Sequels rarely live up to their forebears. Artists always struggle with their sophomore album. But Urbit is a deep well with always more water to draw, and this issue of *USTJ* showcases more of the ramifications of truly solid-state computing.

Since our first issue laid out aspects of the development of Urbit's kernel and userspace, the core development team has been hard at work on accelerating Urbit's processing speed, both the evaluation of Nock and the communications network.

As we wrote in the last issue, "There are deep and true things that can be said about the platonic Urbit, the diamond Urbit, but much of what we are working through now is a contingent Urbit, feeling our way towards zero kelvin." It's never quiet on Mars, but it is slowly cooling.

To the extent modest themes have emerged in this issue, the nature of identity and the structure of Azimuth as a public-key infrastructure are explored; aspects of Clay and Eyre as vanes of Arvo are expounded upon; and several historically important documents have been restored from gists and blog posts to a more permanent record.

We particularly invite readers to engage authors with technical commentary at the Urbit Systems Technical Journal Forum.

```
https://journal.urbitsystems.tech/forum.
```

We trust that the reader will find this issue as illuminating as its predecessor and its successors.

Computer science happens in the trenches. ⊠

Designing a Permanent Personal Identity: The Public Key Infrastructure Idea Maze

Phillip C. Monk ~`wicdev-wisryt`
Tlon Corporation

Abstract

Public key infrastructures solve a coordination problem for communicators on a network. Urbit's PKI (Azimuth) is designed to provide globally consistent, permanent, and completely self-owned identities. This post explores the design choices that led to Urbit's PKI, including the trade-offs between impermanence and self-attestation, global consistency, and scalability. Urbit's PKI includes three types of names epitomizing the poles of the tradeoff trilemma.

A public key infrastructure (PKI) is a system for binding a set of keys to a name. Sometimes a small amount of metadata is included. Existing PKIS include PGP-style "web of trust", SSL certificates, ZeroTier, Keybase, OpenID, Mozilla Persona, and Login with Google. These take unique approaches to the problem and have achieved some degree of success, but none provide globally consistent, permanent, and completely self-owned identities. In this article, we will describe Urbit's approach to achieving these properties in its PKI.

Urbit's PKI is named "Azimuth" (or occasionally "Urbit ID"). Azimuth is Urbit's identity layer, built as a suite of smart contracts on the Ethereum blockchain and several apps run locally on your "ship". (In Urbit, a "name" is often called a "ship" or

Urbit Systems Technical Journal I:2 (2024): 1–7.

Address author correspondence to ~wicdev-wisryt

an "address" because we use the metadata in the PKI to make names routable.) The total data is two 256-bit asymmetric keys, a cryptographic suite number (to allow changing crypto algorithms), the revision number of the key, and the name of a ship that will route for it. This sums to less than 128 bytes of data.

Each PKI trades off various properties. We chose a tripartite system so that appropriate choices can be made for different use cases. Here, we explore the various properties we chose by following a series of binary choices—the idea maze.

One way to classify PKIs is by permanence: either you can change your keys or not. If you cannot, then your name is impermanent, for no one can keep a set of keys secure forever. Even if your opsec never fails, eventually your crypto algorithms may be compromised.

However, if you sacrifice the ability to change your keys, you can achieve a very nice property: self-attesting keys. If your name is a hash of your public key information, then no other source of information is required to verify you are who you say you are. This is a useful property since it requires no coordination at all. Many things are impermanent, especially during development. It also provides a way to try out the network without obtaining a permanent address.

This is our first stop in the idea maze. We call this sort of name a "comet". A comet's name is the 128-bit hash of its public keys.[1]

However, Urbit is yours and it's forever. You shouldn't have to change your name every time you change your keys. So, we go back and take the other choice: you must be able to change your keys.

To change keys, you must sign a message with the old keys revoking them and supplying the new ones[2]. The question is what happens if the old keys also sign a second set of new keys. This could happen if an attacker obtained your old keys after

---

[1]We currently limit comets to "sponsors", particular stars which are whitelisted to create them. This is a matter of policy and not inherent to the PKI design.

[2]Or the equivalent with a hierarchical key structure. In practice, you want to have a master key which signs a junior key for everyday use. You use the master key to rotate the junior key.

the fact. This is important because one of the reasons to be able to change your keys is to invalidate the old ones so that they have no power.

We have two options again: the PKI may be globally consistent or not. To be globally consistent means that if you believe a name is bound to a set of keys, then nobody on the network will disagree.

If you don't require global consistency, you may sign this message and send it to all your neighbors, and they pass it on, and hopefully it gets to most of the network quickly. However, if one of those ships receives two contradictory versions of this message, the only thing it can do is trust the first one it heard, which may be different than what someone else heard. Thus, this is pairwise consistent but globally inconsistent. This is essentially how the pre-blockchain Ames network worked, though key changes were not actually implemented. Because global consistency is a valuable property, we looked at other options.

For a globally consistent PKI that allows you to revoke keys, you need to be able to distinguish between two cryptographically valid messages to determine which was signed first. The dual problem could be solved easily — you can prove a message is signed after another by including the signature of the first in the second. This is equivalent to reading out a newspaper headline to prove a message was recorded after a given day.

However, the problem of proving one message was sent before any later ones inverts the problem. You can solve this with newspapers by placing the message in the text of the newspaper. However, while reading a newspaper requires no central party, writing one does. For a long time, this sort of message was always handled by a central party. SSL revocations are managed by a few central parties. When you buy property, it's not sufficient to have the previous owner sign the title — this must be entered into a central land registry. Otherwise, the owner may sell their property to multiple people and there would be no way to determine who is the new owner. With the land registry, all you need to do is ask the registry which sale happened first, and that's the one that counts.

However, Urbit is yours and it's forever. Trusting central registries jeopardizes both. The keen reader will notice that the problem of determining which key rotation happened first is exactly the double-spend problem that Satoshi solved with his proof of work algorithm for Bitcoin. His first block famously includes a newspaper headline to prove he didn't mine the block before that date. In a beautiful duality, his own algorithm proves that he didn't mine it after that date.[3]

Some argue that blockchain is only good for money. This is myopic and is generally based on the experience that its most valuable application so far has been money. However, blockchain is a cryptographic primitive to do what was previously impossible: prove that one message was signed before another without a central party. Blockchain was discovered by someone trying to create digital money, and he needed that primitive, but that doesn't mean that's all it's good for.

Thus, we store our PKI data on a blockchain for our second kind of name: planets. A planet is a 32-bit address which has key information stored on the blockchain.[4] The owner of a planet may broadcast new PKI data by adding it to the blockchain. Any later messages by the old keys will be rejected, and everyone on the network will listen to the blockchain for key data. Thus, we have global consistency, permanence, and self sovereignty. We know of no other solution that can provide these properties.

However, while small individually, the aggregate PKI data for all nodes on the network may become very large. This is not an issue for comets because nobody needs to store comet keys except for those which they're talking with, and even those can be garbage-collected and re-requested and verified. For planets, there is a canonical set of keys, and somebody must store that. There are about 232, or 4 billion planets. If the PKI

---

[3]More strictly: it proves that he didn't mine it after the other blocks currently on the Bitcoin blockchain. It only gives an ordering within the chain, not a literal timestamp. But cf. Gigi (2019) and particularly Gigi (2021) on Bitcoin ordering as time.

[4]In addition to planets, there are stars and galaxies. From a PKI perspective they're treated exactly like planets, but on the network they provide infrastructure services like routing.

data is about 100 bytes for each planet, this is about 400 GB of data. This may be more than most users wish to store, but it's small enough that it would be very cheap for someone to host this data for many users.[5]

This information is currently stored directly on the Ethereum blockchain, but as is well understood in blockchain circles this approach will not scale beyond a certain point. Many chains are pursuing designs that allow the users of the smart contracts to locally store the data associated with the contracts they care about and only commit hashes to the chain. We expect there to be several viable options for this by the time Azimuth's scaling needs exceed what's provided by Ethereum. This will free us from the cost of hosting the PKI data on all Ethereum nodes, but the data must still be stored somewhere. Any service that could handle such a large amount of data would inherently centralize the network. Azimuth and Jael make reference to an external source of truth for their own and peer's key information, but do not otherwise depend on Ethereum for their operation.

However, 4 billion is not enough addresses for every device on the planet today, much less in a few decades. So, we apply our maxim of re-examining our choices at each level for each use case. Examining the idea maze above, we cannot use the blockchain option for everything since the data is too big. However, it's not actually necessary for each of your devices to have its own self-sovereign identity separate from your planet. So we choose the option of using a central registry: your own planet.

We allocate 4 billion "moons" to each of those planets. A moon is a 64-bit address whose 32-bit suffix is its planet. Your planet can easily store the keys for its own moons, and anyone who needs to talk to your moons can ask you for the keys. This is the sense in which moons are true ships: they're permanent names and you own them completely, as long as you own the planet. However, they're not independent ships — their keys can always be revoked by their planet.

---

[5]In practice, this will likely be an included service by your sponsoring star. It should never rise above the capital cost of a 400GB hard drive.

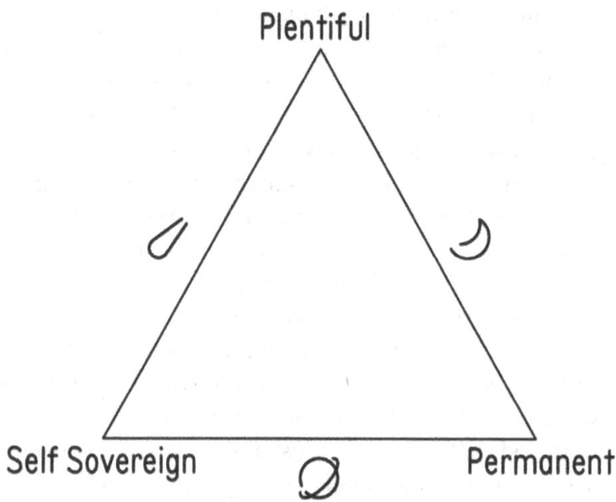

Figure 1: Trilemma of properties for a sane network.

To create a sane network, we require global consistency for all our names (Figure 1). There are three other properties; pick any two:

- Comets are impermanent, self sovereign, and plentiful.

- Planets are permanent, self sovereign, and not plentiful.

- Moons are permanent, not self sovereign, and plentiful.

Fancifully, comets are wayward celestial bodies that are great for testing and miscellaneous low-value things that won't last for long. Planets are where you can build a home and shape it into anything you want it to be. People can always find your planet; it's not going anywhere. Moons are useful for special purposes, like storage, heavy industry, and anything else you might want to do off-planet.[6] ⚘

---

[6]To extend the metaphor, stars are a neighborhood to live in—they're easier for other planets to see, so when they want to send you a message they look for your star first. If they don't even know where your star is, they can certainly

References

Gigi (2019). *21 Lessons: What I've Learned from Falling Down the Bitcoin Rabbit Hole*. Independently published. URL:
```
https://www.amazon.com/gp/product/1697526349/ref=
as_li_tl?ie=UTF8&camp=1789&creative=9325&
creativeASIN=1697526349&linkId=
b17de885d1dfaf3cec52479f69374fbb
```
(visited on ~2024.3.7).

— (2021) "Bitcoin is Time". URL:
```
https://dergigi.com/2021/01/14/bitcoin-is-time/
```
(visited on ~2024.3.7).

---

find your star's galaxy, and that will be enough to locate the star. Of course, if your star is not providing satisfactory service, you can take your planet and move to another star.

On the Utility of Azimuth and Decentralized Identity

Stuart Christoph ~sarlev-sarsen
~tocwex.syndicate

Abstract

This article considers the concept of identity within the context of Urbit and its identity layer, Azimuth. Comparison is made to self-sovereign identity (SSI) and decentralized identity (DID) design principles. We consider how these systems implement decentralized identity, examining their technical foundations, practical applications, and the broader implications for digital self-sovereignty. Understanding these elements sheds light on the future of identity in a decentralized world.

Contents

Urbit Systems Technical Journal I:2 (2024): 1–7.
Address author correspondence to ~wicdev-wisryt

1 Introduction

The nature of identity has captivated human attention since prehistory. Cave painting self-portraits and handprints reveal an early sense of 'self' in even the earliest hominids. More recently, Descartes' *cogito, ergo sum* laid the groundwork for modern philosophy. As we move into the digital age, the concept of 'identity' continues to evolve in order to extend into online networks.

This article considers the concept of identity within the context of Urbit and its identity layer, Azimuth. We explore how these systems implement decentralized identity, examining their technical foundations, practical applications, and the broader implications for digital self-sovereignty. By understanding these elements, we aim to shed light on the future of identity in a decentralized world.

1.1   Decentralized Identity

Urbit isn't the only project working on the concept of decentralized identity. As a starting point, we will examine two perspectives on decentralized identity:

1. Self-Sovereign Identity

2. Decentralized Identifiers

Blockchain developer Christopher Allen coined the term 'self-sovereign identity' (ssi) to concretize a notion of digital decentralized identity built for individual control and self-determination (Allen, 2016). He noted that the evolution of online identity has passed through eras of centralized administrative control, oligarchic federated systems, and unfortunately, institutionally captured "user-centric" designs. The next era, designated the era of ssi, thankfully aims to return us to a more intuitive understanding of digital identity. Allen defined ten key principles for ssi:[1]

- Existence
- Control
- Access
- Transparency
- Persistence
- Portability
- Interoperability
- Consent
- Minimalization
- Protection

However, we contend that each of the pre-ssi eras has critically pulled us away from the sense of 'self' that is vital to identity–from the way we experience our identity in the world of atoms and the digital experiences which are becoming ingrained in our day-to-day lives.

Separate from Allen's principles, w3c has presented a standard for Decentralized Identifiers (DIDs). According to "Decentralized Identifiers (DIDs) v1.0", in part (World Wide Web Consortium, 2022):

> Decentralized identifiers (DIDs) are a new type of identifier that enables verifiable, decentralized digital identity. A DID refers to any subject (e. g. a person, organization, thing, data model, abstract

____

[1] The appendix contains an excerpt defining the principles more completely.

entity, etc.) as determined by the controller of the
DID. ...

While other parties might be used to help enable
the discovery of information related to a DID, the
design enables the controller of a DID to prove control over it without requiring permission from any
other party. DIDs are URIs that associate a DID subject with a DID document allowing trustable interactions associated with that subject.

While the Urbit project may not traditionally rely on 'Earth
standards,' the DID recommendation also defines ten design
goals that are informative for understanding decentralized
identity.[2]

- Decentralization
- Control
- Privacy
- Security
- Proof-based
- Discoverability
- Interoperability
- Portability
- Simplicity
- Extensibility

We will revisit some of these principles and design goals
in the context of Azimuth and Urbit, but first, a reminder to
developers: defaults matter.

1.2   Defaults Matter

As ~wicdev-wisryt noted of the public key infrastructure (PKI)
idea maze (see ~wicdev-wisryt (2024), pp. 1–7 in this issue),
the long history of PKIs largely splits between being 'decentralized and unused' or 'centralized and easy to subject oneself to'.
~wicdev-wisryt explored this idea maze along the branches of
global consistency, permanence, and self-ownership, to which
we add a fourth branch: sane defaults.

PGP, GPG, and Web of Trust solutions have existed for
decades but are used by effectively nobody, and in some sense
can be dismissed due to a lack of sane defaults. One could argue the shortcoming of these systems is a lack of global consistency, but in practice global consistency is a necessary but

---

[2]See the appendix for a more complete excerpt explicating the design goals

not sufficient condition for a self-sovereign identity. If the system does not also provide sane defaults the global consistency remains an illegible mess to the typical user. The Web of Trust and similar solutions may be glossed over as demonstrably insufficient thanks to this shortcoming.

If we consider global consistency, permanence, and self-ownership as useful goals for the PKI, we must recognize that they fail to explain some of the more controversial elements of Azimuth's hierarchical model for a certain subset of critics. In fact, alternate conceptions for PKIs and identity more broadly are being explored by both Kinode[3] and Pallas.[4] These projects aim to satisfy each of the three branches but take different approaches to the concept of sane defaults. So why does Urbit's Azimuth retain a hierarchical address space?

Aside from being a clean way of naming a finite address space, Azimuth's hierarchy provides a *sane default* for packet routing, peer discovery, and third-party service provision. It gives users a starting point, and a set of alternatives that are tractable. It serves as the crisis moment ('It's dangerous to go alone! Take this') before embarking on the journey of self-sovereign identity.

Some critics frame this structure as 'digital feudalism' but fail to understand two other elements of the system:

1. The default PKI includes a permissionless right to exit, requiring no approval from the network node up the hierarchy from you.

2. Even the hierarchical model is *just a sane default* and does not forbid an alternative.

While no alternative exists at present,[5] there is no reason that a particular Urbit ship must exclusively ask its sponsor for the

---

[3] As of writing, Kinode's .os identity implementation leans towards allowing users to bring their own identity system, and handling packet routing by designated and self-declared routing nodes.

[4] As of writing, Pallas, formerly Plunder, has not implemented an identity system. In the author's conversations with developers working on the project, Pallas aims to be unopinionated about either identity system or packet routing and peer discovery, instead deferring that role to projects building on top of the system.

[5] As a last minute addition, we note the "Groundwire" proposal (by

addresses of its peers. Nor is there any technical restriction on Urbit's routing packets using a different model. In summary, *the hierarchy is a sane default in an otherwise infinite game.*

2   The Current State of Azimuth

The need to place the PKI on a distributed ledger with global consensus and recognize the hierarchical model as a sane default is obvious. But what about the current address space and its technical implementation? Since early 2019, Azimuth has been on hosted on the Ethereum blockchain, and in 2022 the contracts were updated to support a "naive" Layer 2 rollup. Returning to the principles and design goals of SSI and DIDs, this on-chain presence provides benefits such as existence, control, transparency, persistence, decentralization, and discoverability. It also supports many of the other stated goals, if not satisfying them purely through an on-chain presence. Many of these principles were either explicitly or implicitly considered with both the initial Azimuth contracts (~ravmel-ropdyl, 2019), and the move to supporting the Layer 2 rollup (~datnut-pollen, 2021). However, the current state of Azimuth falls short in terms of providing interoperability and extensibility.

2.1   Layer 1 IDs on the Ethereum network

Azimuth's deployment on Ethereum was one of the first uses of the ERC-721 standard (Entriken et al., 2018). It is implemented across two core contracts: Azimuth, which holds the registry of identity ownership, and Ecliptic, which defines the business logic for updating the state of the registry. To this day, these contracts serve as one of the most technically 'useful' ERC-721s on the Ethereum network, powering the peer-to-peer interactions of thousands of nodes (also known as urbit ships) in an

---

~hastuc-dibtux, ~tondes-sitrym, et al.), which was published just before this issue went to print. Groundwire suggested a project for a Gall agent enabling usage of Bitcoin and the comet level address space for an alternative PKI without hard-forking Azimuth.

encrypted off-chain network. As an ERC-721, Urbit ID experienced a significant increase in valuation during the NFT boom of 2021, with the market cap of address space breaking \$2B at its peak.

However, the core downside of Azimuth's presence on Ethereum should not be understated. In exchange for the benefits of NFT hype cycles, Urbit users must pay a tax to the Ethereum network in the form of gas fees. This interaction can be particularly expensive because the original versions of Ecliptic required all state transition computations to occur on-chain. While this means Azimuth inherits the security benefits of Ethereum's global consensus model, there is a contention that it fundamentally extracts value from the Urbit network and deposits it into Ethereum in an unnecessary exchange.

2.2   Layer 2 IDs on the naive rollup

The transaction costs on Ethereum were so great that, at times, it cost over \$200 worth of ETH just to get on the network. For a budding distributed system project, such costs can be unbearable. Thus, the solution to the 'gas crisis' was introduced (`~datnut-pollen`, 2021): a custom 'naive' rollup. The key feature of the naive rollup is that, instead of paying Ethereum miners (now validators) to verify the state transitions of Azimuth, each Urbit node can validate those transitions themselves. This again brings us back to the idea of sane defaults in a decentralized or distributed network.

That is, in running one's Urbit instance, the canonical "Azimuth" is nothing more than a sane default. This is trivially exemplified by the fact that one could run a fake ship network locally and act as any Urbit ID one chose, or even deploy an alternative version of Azimuth onto mainnet Ethereum. However, because everyone else is likely operating on the default version of `/app/azimuth`, which assumes `azimuth.eth` as The One True PKI, any of one's potential peers will discard one's packets as invalid. The Urbit network will ignore an unsignable interloper. Whether or not the Urbit network pays the Ethereum network for state transition computation, it remains true that Urbit's off-chain interactions are voluntary and governed by sane defaults.

2.3   When to Use Global Consensus

As noted in ~wicdev-wisryt's piece, blockchains allow users to distinguish two cryptographically valid messages, specifically which was signed first, without requiring a centralized party. Both Layer 1 and Layer 2 implementations rely on this affordance. Effectively, they both need the chain to give them a timestamp and a signed message to discern key ownership. Whether the cosmputation of key rotation is done on-chain or client side, anyone within the Urbit network that is continuing to use the system defaults will ultimately get the correct result for validating a packet's sender. It is the core affordance of timestamped messages for which Urbit must pay *some* blockchain to have a viable decentralized PKI.

However, Urbit-side key validation and peer discovery are not the only benefits of having the PKI on Ethereum. The cost of on-chain computation for global consensus is undoubtedly a hurdle to low-cost user adoption of Urbit. However, it would be a failure of imagination to claim there is no contingent loss of benefits. Specifically, Ethereum is a growing network that is building on top of the same ERC-721 standard on which Urbit ID is defined. Improvements to the capabilities of the Ethereum network can enhance the capabilities of the Urbit network—*if Urbit maintains, or increases, its legibility to the Ethereum Network.* The current naive rollup does not achieve this. An L2 Urbit ID, and it's ownership in particular, is functionally illegible to the outside world. From the perspective of Ethereum, global consistency is compromised, and key rotation is impossible to validate.

While we could explore the technical details of these two systems, instead let's return to examine the SSI principles and DID design goals of interoperability and extensibility. In a sense, these just mean that you want your identity to work in as many places as possible. To be as legible to as many systems or stakeholders as is possible.

A playful example of this is whether one would trade one's state-issued driver's license for a high school ID card (~sarlev-sarsen, 2024). In spite of one's driver's license being more costly to replace or update, one's response is almost certainly, "No way." A licensee knows intuitively that a driver's license is a more credible and legible identifier than a high school ID, in large part due to the authority of the centralized issuing authority. Imagine achieving such a level of credibility and legibility in a self-sovereign manner. This tradeoff is not merely a thought experiment, as dependency on centralized identity issuance authorities has real world impacts:

> In the last year, self-sovereign identity has also entered the sphere of *international policy*. This has largely been driven by the refugee crisis that has beset Europe, which has resulted in many people lacking a recognized identity due to their flight from the state that issued their credentials. However, it's a long-standing international problem, as foreign workers have often been abused by the countries they work in due to the lack of state-issued credentials. (Allen, 2016)

One may reasonably ask at this junction whether, if Urbit IDs will form the foundation for self-sovereign digital identity, they should be more legible or less legible?

While this may run counter to some Urbit purists who want to avoid anything related to 'Earth code,' the reality for the foreseeable future is that interoperability with other networks is both desirable and necessary for Urbit's continued survival. With time, as Urbit evolves, it may become the most legible system, and the cruft of Earth code will fall by the wayside. But that future is still a long way off.

Improving legibility, or in other words, protecting the interoperability and extensibility of Urbit ID, does not imply loyalty to any particular chain. It simply claims that increasing legibility to the largest set of networks should be included in the objective function of Urbit ID.

3   Alternative Options for the PKI

How does Urbit continue to improve the utility of Azimuth? While in 2019 the options for hosting the PKI were still limited, the technology landscape has drastically evolved in the intervening years. Several Urbit-related blockchain projects have been proposed and explored recently which bear on how the PKI could be hosted in the future.

3.1   Self-Host the PKI on `%chain`

The most 'philosophically straightforward' answer would be for Urbit to self-host its PKI. While this requires further technical development, it is conceptually tractable and the `%chain` project, primarily executed by `~tiller-tolbus` and `~midsum-salrux` as a skunkworks effort, has shown initial successes on implementing an Urbit-native blockchain. This option could make use of identity-backed consensus models, and would be the most direct pathway to the Urbit network not having to pay a 'tax' to another network for its consensus mechanism. In a sense, this is the most 'independent' or 'self-contained' option. However, it would likely result in decreased capital access and practical legibility to external networks.

While reasonable minds may differ on the net benefit of Urbit's proximity to the Ethereum network's capital pools, there is no doubt that such proximity has materially impacted on address space valuation. This includes the ~\$33,000 peak for star-level identities. Distancing Urbit ID from Ethereum by moving the PKI to a self-hosted network would limit the opportunity to access this capital by increasing the barriers to exchange.

Moving the PKI in this way would also decrease interoperability and extensibility by making it harder for the Ethereum network to access and validate data about ownership of Urbit IDs. Technically speaking, this constraint could be reduced by self-hosted RPC endpoints of `%chain` or Azimuth state that could be accessed over HTTP. However, the more prominent issue would be the coordination constraint it would generate. If the PKI moves, what motivation do members of the Ethereum

Network have to bother with Urbit RPC endpoints instead of just staying within the Ethereum tooling ecosystem?

In a world in which Urbit is more powerful and offers a compelling, market-legible alternative to the Ethereum virtual machine, one can see the draw of a bootstrapped %chain. However, the ~\$70,000 per year in gas fees that Urbit users collectively pay to maintain the PKI on Ethereum seems a worthwhile exchange for the legibility it affords.

3.2   Zenith: UrbitChain on Cosmos SDK

Moving the PKI to a self-hosted, urbit-native solution is not the only option should the Urbit network want to reduce its dependency on outside networks. One standing proposal, Zenith, establishes an off-Urbit blockchain governed by the galaxy-level address space and implemented as its own L2 Ethereum rollup using the Cosmos SDK.

In terms of legibility, this pathway essentially splits the difference. The Cosmos ecosystem is smaller than Ethereum as a whole, but comes in second place on metrics for current Total Value Locked (TVL) (Fernau, 2022). The Cosmos ecosystem and SDK could give some of the benefits of a self-hosted system. For example, it would reduce the outflow of capital from the Urbit network, while still achieving some interoperability with the external world thanks to the affordances granted by Cosmos. Peg zones and the Inter-Blockchain Communication (IBC) protocol would enable ready access to a network of blockchain networks. These networks are likely to have more operational friction for capital flows than remaining on L1 Ethereum, but may be a valid tradeoff. Additionally, the Zenith proposal makes a nod to the opportunity to use the Zenith rollup as a general purpose urbit-aware smart contracting platform, including a "Scry Oracle Contract" which would enable canonization of certain subsets of the scry namespace and create some on-chain enforcement mechanisms of the referentially transparent nature of the urbit namespace.

3.3   Mayflower: A Recolonization Effort

Also presented as an option for the future of the Azimuth PKI is a proposal under the codename "Mayflower". While there is currently a directional debate between the Zenith and Mayflower plans, due to disagreements on implementation and design of related non-fungible tokens and governing bodies, the Mayflower proposal similarly suggests use of an Ethereum L2 rollup and visions of future urbit native gas tokens and contracts.[6] The two main distinctions at this time appear to be a preference to avoid 'rolling your own' rollup and leaning towards something like the existing Base rollup and Optimism Superchain, plus a focus on 'rezoning' urbit address space, such that more focused development will occur within the readily available 'digital land'. Proponents of this plan have noted that it neither precludes an Urbit-native chain, nor path to an Urbit specific rollup. As of writing, specific details on this plan are outstanding and in active debate. Notably, both these proposals aim towards using existing Ethereum layer 2 technology, but depending on implementation details the portability of identities between L1 and L2 is undetermined.

3.4   Bridge the PKI across multiple chains

As we consider the tradeoffs of moving the PKI, it is worth revisiting our 'sane defaults' branch in the idea maze. If `azimuth.eth` and with it `/app/azimuth.hoon`[7] are just sane defaults, why not also support some sane *alternatives*? One of the final Urbit precepts reminds us that "communities are autonomous" (~wicdev-wisryt, 2020).

To this end, we should use Urbit OS as the coordination technology to allow users and communities to decide with which other networks they desire to maintain legibility. As with the current PKI's split between L1 Ethereum and the naive rollup, so too could we allow people to move their Urbit ID

---

[6] The author of this piece makes no statement about the financial viability of these two options and notes that they both appear to recognize the illegibility of the way the PKI is currently fractured and aim at rectifying it.

[7] The Jael secrets vane of Urbit OS merely subscribes for the PKI state, rather than storing it in Arvo itself.

from L1 Ethereum to any other chain with a viable way to post signature data.

Some may choose to remain on mainnet Ethereum to take advantage of features like ERC-6551 Token Bound Account (Windle et al., 2023).[8] Others may want to inscribe their ownership as an Ordinal on Bitcoin. Alternatively, Solana offers some benefits for the more crypto-degenerate who are looking for speed of trading and market volatility to help make their wealth.

Considering this path, it is worthwhile to elaborate on how the current L2 solution works. The original version of the Ethereum contracts held ownership data in the Azimuth contracts and business logic in the Ecliptic contracts. In 2021, these contracts were updated to support two new affordances:

- Azimuth points sent to the Ethereum deposit address (`0x1111...`) are assessed by the default Urbit client as being owned on layer 2.

- Ecliptic posts *time-stamped* signature data to the Ethereum chain concerning the change of ownership of a point owned on layer 2. The default Urbit client reviews and validates the state change before applying the change to the Urbit's own `/app/azimuth`.

This mechanism means that these points are still cryptographically controlled for purposes of anyone running the default Urbit OS or relevant code (namely, `/app/eth-watcher`, `/lib/naive.hoon`, `/app/azimuth-tracker` and `/app/azimuth`), and it is easy to imagine how this same mechanism could be used to support other chains as hosts for portions of the PKI:

1. Define a holding address for the ERC-721 on mainnet ethereum for other host chains (i. e. sending the L1 NFT to `0x2222...` indicates sending the ownership to Bitcoin).

---

[8] ERC-6551 implements an interface and registry for smart contract accounts deterministically controlled by one's ERC-721 Urbit ID.

2. Implement a watcher for the subject chain that looks for posted signature data.

3. Update and/or add to the relevant Urbit OS code for client side validation of data posted to the new chain.

This approach would increase legibility to other chains, giving communities more options for what their members can achieve with their Urbit ID.

However, as the PKI fractures, maintaining global consistency becomes increasingly complex. In the above model, the primary solution for maintaining this consistency becomes that official 'global consensus' is on mainnet Ethereum, while any other alternative is subject only to the client side validation. Depending on the affordances of the subject chain, the level of effort put into building the subsystem, and any cost concerns for network fees on the specific subject chain, the result is likely that *moving to any other chain is a one-way trip.* Just as a move to the current naive rollup is a one way trip.

The biggest reason for this being the case is the question: 'what timestamp is the canonical one?'.

3.5   Move the PKI to Nockchain

While Ethereum has made significant progress in interchain bridges and L2 rollups since the implementation of the Naive rollup, making two-way bridges increasingly possible, they still introduce a host of security and consensus questions. They also are likely to exacerbate the capital outflow concerns of the current L1 Ethereum implementation.

But if we return to the philosophical perspective, assuming we want our identities to be legible to different networks, don't we also want to potentially modify that legibility? Just as individuals can emigrate between nation-states, it seems self-evident that we should be able to move between digital networks, bringing our self-sovereign identities with us.

What is the best way to enable this portability (another shared principle/design goal for SSIS/DIDS) while maintaining global consistency? The reader who is familiar with Nockchain will anticipate the punchline: zero-knowledge proofs.

Using Zorp's EDEN and its associated Nock prover (~tacryp-socryt et al., 2023), any Urbit instance can prove valid computation of any 'client-side' Azimuth state change and use that proof as the data to post to any given blockchain. It is likely that the 'easiest' place to do that would be Nockchain. However, external legibility may incentivize these proofs to be posted elsewhere. An Azimuth contract on a subject chain could use the proof of valid Nock computation to assign ownership of an Urbit ID crypto-asset native to a given address. This could include whatever affordances native asset ownership on that chain may bestow to an Urbit operator.

In the long run, this pathway would likely lead more Urbit operators to move their Urbit ID's primary 'citizenship' to Nockchain. This would occur without unnecessarily losing legibility to other networks, and retains the possibility of absorbing external capital into the Urbit network along the way.

4   Other Considerations for Azimuth

While Azimuth's on-chain nature is that of a public key infrastructure, a PKI alone does not constitute a complete identity system. In fact, it is the pairing of Urbit ID with Urbit OS that presents the best opportunity to serve as a fully-fledged decentralized identity system. Whether we look at implementing W3C's standardized DIDs, or adhering to the principles of SSIs, not everything about Azimuth is, or should be, on-chain.

4.1   GroundWire, comets, and Bitcoin Ordinals

An early design consideration of the 21e8 Bitcoin Ordinals project (Ordinals, 2024) was reportedly to be able to host an Azimuth-like PKI system, and the desire to tie Urbit's fortunes more closely to those of Bitcoin persists in segments of the Urbit community. A recent debate throughout the ecosystem about the Azimuth PKI, namely between Zenith and Mayflower, has instigated a wide-ranging discussion about alternative ways of handling identiy across the Urbit network. GroundWire proposes to experiment with both new PKI governance models, and to make use of the comet-level address space in a more robust way (~hastuc-dibtux et al., 2024). Implementation details are still forthcoming, but the initial plan is to prototype a Gall agent to support a PKI on Bitcoin that would allow comets to rotate their keys (updating the current 'self-attestation' model), and make use of different non-hierarchical models for routing and peer-discovery. Additionally, instead of using the finite 'higher level' address space for spam resistance, this proposal would use mechanisms like L1 Bitcoin fee costs, or burning and timelocking coins.

As with the Zenith and Mayflower proposals, the Ground-Wire proposal makes statements about the governance and fundrasing directions of the Urbit project. These topics are out of scope for the focus of this article, but merit ongoing discussion in the appropriate forums.

4.2   Illegible subnets

Globally available and transparent chain state greatly enhances legibility. Openly available sponsorship hierarchies inform unconnected peers about how to reach you, and global claims can be used for various purposes. However, not every application requires global consensus, and Turing-complete smart contracts can lead to the risk of open-ended cost overruns. Furthermore, many networks may wish to become or remain illegible to the outside world. Private access control lists, gossip networks, and packet routing mechanisms enable use cases that would not benefit from the cost or transparency of on-chain or globally consistent legibility.[9] Urbit's off-chain and encrypted peer-to-peer messaging affordances open up an intriguing landscape of 'illegible subnets' while still benefiting from associations with specific pseudonymous Urbit identities.

The value of illegible subnets also builds on the insight that not everything can, or should, be distilled down to its lowest common denominator, tokenized, and put on the blockchain.

---

[9]It is worth noting that illegible subnets may contend with the SSI principle of consent, in that they enable opaque data-sharing networks and other similar 'darknet' use cases.

The more complex the interaction, the more costly the distillation process, and *the more likely there is no consensus to be found around its 'valuation'*. Instead of demanding timestamped global consensus in all our peer interactions, we must support emergent, implied-consensus networks. These networks are governed not by immutable chain state but by willing association and participation by sovereign peers. Systems where the network forms and dissolves on the fly, based on the ongoing discovery and refinement of the values of its participants.

4.3   Peer-to-peer attestations

Another affordance that does not require a blockchain is peer-to-peer attestation. There are many use cases where the privacy and cost benefits of cryptographically verifiable peer-to-peer attestations are desirable. They can be used independently, e. g. "`~sarlev-sarsen` attests to having received a message from `~lagrev-nocfep` containing a valid passcode", or even in conjunction with global blockchain state.

For example, `%fund` by `~tocwex.syndicate`,[10] uses peer-to-peer attestation begin to build a subjective reputation graph. An Urbit can hold a signed message from an Ethereum wallet attesting contol, e. g. "`~sarlev-sarsen` controls wallet `0x6789...`", and can even share this signed message with other peers.

```
::  $prof: user profile data
::
++  prof
  $:  ship-url=@t
      wallets=(map addr sigm)
      favorites=(set flag)
  ==
::
```

 Anyone receiving that attestation can then use it in constructing an understanding of the relationships between different Urbit IDs, off-chain financial promises, on-chain transactions,

---

[10]`https://tocwexsyndicate.com`

reputation, or other economic activity, without it thereby becoming a canonical, globally available understanding.

Such shared understandings granted by peer-to-peer attestations can thus create pockets of privileged information networks, and the attendant competitive advantages of a more opaque, yet verifiable, system.

4.4   Self-verified credentials

As ~wicdev-wisryt notes, one offshoot of the permanence branch of the PKI idea maze makes available a mechanism for self-attestation. This currently only exists for the portion of Azimuth's address space where comet identities reside. This self-attestation is useful for a variety of purposes—cost, anonymity, etc.—but doesn't afford a more long-lasting system for self-verified credentials due to the transient nature of a comet identity. It is likely that expanding the capacity for self-attestations would be of benefit to the Urbit network. In particular, the concept of Verifiable Credentials (VC) may be worth pursuing (World Wide Web Consortium, 2022).

Urbit ID does not currently have a system of verifiable credentials, and arguably, the PKI aspect of Azimuth should never include this. However, it should be reasonably straightforward to produce either a VC attestation layer utilizing Azimuth or incorporate knowledge of Azimuth into a VC solution.

One mechanism that could be integrated into an Urbit-native VC solution is the Urbit Hierarchical Deterministic (HD) Wallet. This is the technology used to secure ownership of an Urbit ID point and could satisfy the SSI doctrinal requirement that, "an SSI digital wallet should implement open standards for portable, self-sovereign verifiable credentials and other sensitive private data" (Preukschat and Reed, 2021). Without VC, Urbit does not yet qualify for SSI under this definition.

5   Conclusion

Much work remains to be done on both the on-chain implementations and off-chain affordances of Azimuth and the Urbit ID system. Each area of work must be considered alongside the effort required for implementation:

- Balancing optionality in the PKI for end users against the ongoing maintenance of a more complex codebase.

- Weighing legibility for external networks against measures that reduce capital outflows from the network.

- Allocating development time to adherence with DID, SSI, and VC standards against the practical usefulness of their implementation.

- Coordinating systems for illegible subnets and peer-to-peer attestations against other features that can be productized and marketed to consumers.

Regardless of the specific focus, Urbit ID and the Azimuth address space offer developers a platform to build systems that enhance individual sovereignty and provide flexibility in creating community networks that control their own legibility and interactions.▨

6 Appendix

This appendix serves as a reference for the more complete excerpts of referenced articles.

6.1 The Path to Self-Sovereign Identity

The principles of SSI are as follows ("Ten Principles of Self-Sovereign Identity," 26 April 2016), all quoted:

> A number of different people have written about the principles of identity. Kim Cameron wrote one of the earliest "Laws of Identity", while the aforementioned Respect Network policy and W3C Verifiable Claims Task Force FAQ offer additional perspectives on digital identity. This section draws on all of these ideas to create a group of principles

specific to self-sovereign identity. As with the definition itself, consider these principles a departure point to provoke a discussion about what's truly important.

These principles attempt to ensure the user control that's at the heart of self-sovereign identity. However, they also recognize that identity can be a double-edged sword — usable for both beneficial and maleficent purposes. Thus, an identity system must balance transparency, fairness, and support of the commons with protection for the individual.

1. **Existence**. *Users must have an independent existence.* Any self-sovereign identity is ultimately based on the ineffable "I" that's at the heart of identity. It can never exist wholly in digital form. This must be the kernel of self that is upheld and supported. A self-sovereign identity simply makes public and accessible some limited aspects of the "I" that already exists.

2. **Control**. *Users must control their identities.* Subject to well-understood and secure algorithms that ensure the continued validity of an identity and its claims, the user is the ultimate authority on their identity. They should always be able to refer to it, update it, or even hide it. They must be able to choose celebrity or privacy as they prefer. This doesn't mean that a user controls all of the claims on their identity: other users may make claims about a user, but they should not be central to the identity itself.

3. **Access**. *Users must have access to their own data.* A user must always be able to easily retrieve all the claims and other data within his identity. There must be no hidden data and no gatekeepers. This does not mean that a user can necessarily modify all the claims associated with his identity, but it does mean they should be aware of them. It also does not mean that users have equal access to others' data, only to their own.

4. **Transparency**. *Systems and algorithms must be transparent.* The systems used to administer and operate a network of identities must be open, both in how they function and in how they are managed and updated. The algorithms should be free, open-source, well-known, and as independent as possible of any particular architecture; anyone should be able to examine how they work.

5. **Persistence**. *Identities must be long-lived.* Preferably, identities should last forever, or at least for as long as the user wishes. Though private keys might need to be rotated and data might need to be changed, the identity remains. In the fast-moving world of the Internet, this goal may not be entirely reasonable, so at the least identities should last until they've been outdated by newer identity systems. This must not contradict a "right to be forgotten"; a user should be able to dispose of an identity if he wishes and claims should be modified or removed as appropriate over time. To do this requires a firm separation between an identity and its claims: they can't be tied forever.

6. **Portability**. *Information and services about identity must be transportable.* Identities must not be held by a singular third-party entity, even if it's a trusted entity that is expected to work in the best interest of the user. The problem is that entities can disappear — and on the Internet, most eventually do. Regimes may change, users may move to different jurisdictions. Transportable identities ensure that the user remains in control of his identity no matter what, and can also improve an identity's persistence over time.

7. **Interoperability**. *Identities should be as widely usable as possible.* Identities are of little value if they only work in limited niches. The goal of a 21st-century digital identity system is to make identity information widely available, crossing international boundaries to create global identities, without losing user control. Thanks to persistence

and autonomy these widely available identities can then become continually available.

8. **Consent**. *Users must agree to the use of their identity.* Any identity system is built around sharing that identity and its claims, and an interoperable system increases the amount of sharing that occurs. However, sharing of data must only occur with the consent of the user. Though other users such as an employer, a credit bureau, or a friend might present claims, the user must still offer consent for them to become valid. Note that this consent might not be interactive, but it must still be deliberate and well-understood.

9. **Minimalization**. *Disclosure of claims must be minimized.* When data is disclosed, that disclosure should involve the minimum amount of data necessary to accomplish the task at hand. For example, if only a minimum age is called for, then the exact age should not be disclosed, and if only an age is requested, then the more precise date of birth should not be disclosed. This principle can be supported with selective disclosure, range proofs, and other zero-knowledge techniques, but non-correlatibility is still a very hard (perhaps impossible) task; the best we can do is to use minimalization to support privacy as best as possible.

10. **Protection**. *The rights of users must be protected.* When there is a conflict between the needs of the identity network and the rights of individual users, then the network should err on the side of preserving the freedoms and rights of the individuals over the needs of the network. To ensure this, identity authentication must occur through independent algorithms that are censorship-resistant and force-resilient and that are run in a decentralized manner.

6.2 Decentralized Identifiers (dids) v1.0

The design goals of DIDs are as follows (Section 1.2, "Version 1.0 of the W3C Recommendation 19 July 2022"), all quoted:

1. **Decentralization**. Eliminate the requirement for centralized authorities or single point failure in identifier management, including the registration of globally unique identifiers, public verification keys, services, and other information.

2. **Control**. Give entities, both human and non-human, the power to directly control their digital identifiers without the need to rely on external authorities.

3. **Privacy**. Enable entities to control the privacy of their information, including minimal, selective, and progressive disclosure of attributes or other data.

4. **Security**. Enable sufficient security for requesting parties to depend on DID documents for their required level of assurance.

5. **Proof-based**. Enable DID controllers to provide cryptographic proof when interacting with other entities.

6. **Discoverability**. Make it possible for entities to discover DIDs for other entities, to learn more about or interact with those entities.

7. **Interoperability**. Use interoperable standards so DID infrastructure can make use of existing tools and software libraries designed for interoperability.

8. **Portability**. Be system- and network-independent and enable entities to use their digital identifiers with any system that supports DIDs and DID methods.

9. **Simplicity**. Favor a reduced set of simple features to make the technology easier to understand, implement, and deploy.

10. **Extensibility**. Where possible, enable extensibility provided it does not greatly hinder interoperability, portability, or simplicity.

References

Allen, Christopher (2016) "The Path to Self-Sovereign Identity". URL:
https://www.lifewithalacrity.com/article/the-path-to-self-sovereign-identity/ (visited on ~2024.8.29).

~datnut-pollen, Jonathan Paprocki (2021) "The Gang Solves the Gas Crisis". URL: https://urbit.org/blog/rollups.

Entriken, William et al. (2018) "ERC-721: Non-Fungible Token Standard". URL:
https://eips.ethereum.org/EIPS/eip-721 (visited on ~2024.8.29).

Fernau, Owen (2022) "Cosmos Ecosystem Quietly Surges to $17B in TVL in Challenge to Ethereum Layer 2s". URL:
https://thedefiant.io/news/markets/cosmos-tvl-surge-ethereum.

~hastuc-dibtux, Liam Fitzgerald et al. (2024) "GroundWire 01". URL: https:
//straylight.network/groundwire/groundwire-01 (visited on ~2024.8.29).

Ordinals (2024) "Ordinals Handbook". URL:
https://docs.ordinals.com/ (visited on ~2024.8.29).

Preukschat, Alex and Drummond Reed (2021). *Self-Sovereign Identity: Decentralized digital identity and verifiable credentials*. Manning Publications. ISBN: 9781617296598.

~ravmel-ropdyl, Galen Wolfe-Pauly (2019) "Azimuth is On-Chain". URL:
https://urbit.org/blog/azimuth-is-on-chain.

~sarlev-sarsen, Stuart Cristoph (2024) "Why #l1masterrace is More Than a Meme". URL:
https://sarlev-sarsen.rooftopdao.io/blog/why-l1masterrace-is-more-than-a-meme.

~tacryp-socryt, Logan Allen et al. (2023) "EDEN - a practical, SNARK-friendly combinator VM and ISA". URL: https://eprint.iacr.org/2023/1021.

~wicdev-wisryt, Philip C. Monk (2020) "Urbit Precepts (Discussion)". URL: https://urbit.org/blog/precepts-discussion (visited on ~2024.8.29).

— (2024). "Designing a Permanent Personal Identity: The Public Key Infrastructure Idea Maze." In: *Urbit Systems Technical Journal* 1.2, pp. 1–7.

Windle, Jayden et al. (2023) "ERC-6551: Non-fungible Token Bound Accounts". URL: https://eips.ethereum.org/EIPS/eip-6551 (visited on ~2024.8.29).

World Wide Web Consortium (2022a) "Decentralized Identifiers (DID) v1.0: Core architecture, data model, and representations". URL: https://www.w3.org/TR/did-core/ (visited on ~2024.8.29).

— (2022b) "Verifiable Credentials Data Model 1.1". URL: https://www.w3.org/TR/vc-data-model/ (visited on ~2024.8.29).

Typed Revision Control

N. E. Davis ~`lagrev-nocfep`
Urbit Foundation

Abstract

Contents

1 Introduction

A revision control system[1] is responsible for tracking the state
and history of assets and asset changes within a particular continuity. It may also manage the production of assets through

---

[1] Also "version control system" (vcs); "source control system".

Urbit Systems Technical Journal I:2 (2024): 35–50.
Address author correspondence to ~lagrev-nocfep.

a build system, as used for instance by a continuous integration/continuous deployment (CI/CD) workflow. Trivially, an RCS is a logical filesystem: a database for managing files. (Conventional RCSs are agnostic to the underlying disk hardware, however.[2]) Computer revision control systems have developed from the 1960s onwards once hard drives permitted files to be stored on tape rather than simply as punchcard files. Succeeding generations have introduced new approaches and features, converging more or less on the broad functionality today afforded by Git (Torvalds, 2005) in its elaborated form as a distributed source control system.[3] Much care has been taken to treat the problem of dependencies (e. g. Ball et al. (2015)) and efficient user interfaces (e. g. GitHub, GitLab, etc.). However, although some modest interest has been expressed for a more complete notion of type in revision control, no current system known to the authors besides Urbit's Clay fully implements a typed revision-controlled filesystem. In this article, we explore the approach of current RCSs and elaborate Clay's contributions to the ongoing task of information management and auditable, reproducible source builds.

2   Type in Revision Control Systems

The problem of type in revision control has been of both academic and practical interest for decades (Perry, 1987). Essentially, can file artifacts be organized and classified in such a way as to make them susceptible of comparison across their history? The simplest arrangement which is commonly made is to designate a file as either plaintext or binary. A plaintext file can be updated by specifying the character offset and run length to be replaced (an example of a "diff", or difference between two examples of text; typically these are resolved at the line level rather than character level). Plaintext files, whether ASCII or

---

[2]Compare other logical file systems: network file systems like Microsoft Server Message Block (SMB) drives or distributed file systems like the Hadoop Distributed File System (HDFS) or the InterPlanetary File System (IPFS).

[3]Notably, Git has seemingly failed to fulfill its original promise of being a fully decentralized RCS: most users prefer to use the affordances of centralized Git services such as GitHub or GitLab.

some form of ᴜᴛꜰ, are defined by a regular format with well-understood and predictable symbol widths and offsets. For instance, a little-endian representation of the text `'clay'` would be reproduced in ᴀꜱᴄɪɪ hexadecimal as `0x7961.6c63` and ᴀꜱᴄɪɪ binary as `0b111.1001.0110.0001.0110.1100.0110.0011`. (In binary, each character has a leading zero; that is, each entry is seven bits wide plus a 1-bit zero header.) In contrast, binary files (which is a byword for "everything else") have arbitrary layout and offset; it may be difficult to determine how and why to compare two revisions of any given file. Many ʀᴄꜱꜱ simply treat all registered data as byte streams.

All modern ʀᴄꜱꜱ support plaintext and binary representations of files. Plaintext diffing at the level of line changes is straightforward; the Hunt–McIlroy algorithm is often employed (Hunt and McIlroy, 1976).[4] However, the most popular revision control systems (such as Subversion and Git) have included only minimal direct support for binary diffs. Some systems only support storing successive file copies of a binary file; that is, the diff is the entire deletion of the old file and addition of the new file (e. g. ᴄᴠꜱ). Other systems may support binary file diffs by granular block and offset. Some ʀᴄꜱꜱ support diffing particular binary files using a custom automatic merge tool. For example, the `textconv` tool converts each version of the file to a plaintext representation and compares those representations. (To show a diff for a changes in a ᴘᴅꜰ file, a configured Git instance could compare the text output of `pdfinfo` in each case as a proxy. This is generally legible as metadata but does not of itself include sufficient information to reproduce or reverse the intervening changes; the underlying ʀᴄꜱ still stores the entire binary in its conventional representation.) In any case, type beyond file extension is not generally supported by ʀᴄꜱꜱ; they cannot meaningfully merge files classified as binary.[5]

---

[4] An implementation in Hoon is available at @sigilante/diff.

[5] As always, there are exceptions to the rules. The Git ʀᴄꜱ, for instance, can use a "binary diff" format on exact preimages. The Subversion ʀᴄꜱ does provide an elaborated ᴍɪᴍᴇ support system, wherein users can assign each file a ᴍɪᴍᴇ type that Subversion can use in applying and displaying diffs. However, in practice this only results in the classic text/binary dichotomy with slightly

A general-purpose notion of file type is not isomorphic to conventional type in programming language theory. For instance, consider a JSON file. The following are equivalent as JSON artifacts:

```
{
  "name": "Alice",
  "age": 30
}
```

```
{
  "age": 30,
  "name": "Alice"
}
```

```
{ "name": "Alice", "age": 30, }
```

Indeed, since JSON is structurally agnostic to syntactic whitespace, an infinite number of equivalent files could be constructed. Clearly as plaintext representations, each of these differ, yet they are fully equivalent as JSON artifacts. An RCS which can recognize a JSON input can meaningfully store them as equivalent, while an RCS that makes only the trivial distinction between plaintext and binary must consider them all to be different—nonsemantic changes in structure may trigger spurious diffs in the file's history. Furthermore, a JSON-aware RCS could meaningfully merge these files whereas a plaintext/binary RCS could not. Finally, a JSON-aware RCS could yield a different plaintext output when asked to produce the file, as it could normalize the whitespace to a canonical form. This may be considered by other systems to be an "incorrect" round trip.

Thus we must consider two intersecting notions of file type:

1. The file type as understood by the system, typically based on bitwise reproducibility (e. g. plaintext, binary).

---

more granularity. "Subversion treats all file data as literal byte strings, and files are always stored in the repository in an untranslated state" (Collins-Sussman, Fitzpatrick, and Pilato (2016), section "Binary Files and Translation").

2. The file type as understood conceptually, typically based on structural relationships (e. g. JSON, XML/HTML, Word docx, etc.).

The employment of an intermediate representation allows us to track changes to files and manage their history—state—more effectively. Consider the popular JavaScript framework React (Meta, 2013), aspects of which were developed to resolve difficulties with slow repainting in browsers (for a popular explanation, see Baer (2018), chapter 1). React's virtual Document Object Model (DOM) system acts as an intermediate representation between the actual DOM and the developer's code. When a developer updates the virtual DOM, the framework compares the new virtual DOM with the previous virtual DOM and updates the real DOM only if necessary. This allows React to optimize the rendering process and improve performance. It also means that we can consider the structural representation of the DOM object as an intermediate representation, and the production and application of the diff as a type-aware RCS operation. Higher-level interfaces like Microsoft Word's "Track Changes" feature (Microsoft, 2024) similarly resolves diffs across text and formatting within a document, an artifact processed from a file into a user-friendly representation. While the "Track Changes" user interface is optimized for interactivity, conceptually it is quite similar to conventional merge tools from RCSs, and de facto resolves the same sorts of diffs for its particular file type.[6] Furthermore, the "Source Code in Database" (SCID) approach parses all code into a database as an intermediate representation; this shares some features with a hypothetical type-aware RCS. Thus a significant part of managing typed file data is deciding what the input, output, and diffs should look like, and the remainder is systematic application of these rules to the data.

Given this frame, consider Perry's taxonomy of version control for module interfaces:

---

[6]Indeed, one can imagine a Word-aware command-line RCS that could meaningfully merge changes to a Word document, rather than simply storing successive copies of the file. The OpenDocument file form (odt, ods, odg, etc.) consists of ZIP-compressed XML files, which would be highly amenable to type-aware merge tools at the command line.

1. No version control. Files are simply replaced.

2. Basic version control. Files are versioned with a number, but no diff is applied.

3. Strongly-typed version control. Files are resolved at a structural level, such as procedures or arrays, and diffs are applied at that level.

In this scheme, contemporary Git-style RCS is a "weakly-typed" RCS: the system is aware of versions and diffs, but typically not below the file or line level.[7] Perry was concerned with the behavior and representation of semantic objects, rather than files or data:

> Version equivalence in this type of version control mechanism is defined in terms of syntactic equivalence: data objects are equivalent if their types or structures are equivalent; operations and modules are equivalent if their signatures are equivalent. (Perry, 1987)

Strongly-typed version control requires coupling to the build system, since the system must be aware of the structure of the data in order to apply diffs. (Indeed, ~rovnys-ricfer (2024), pp. 6–7, in USTJ vol. 1 iss. 1, pp. 1–46, discussed one solution to the linking problem which is well-suited to Urbit's global namespace.)

3   Clay

3.1   Revision Control and Marks

Urbit provides the Clay vane at `/sys/vane/clay` to manage Unix-style files and source builds (cf. ~sorreg-namtyv (2016)). Clay acts as both the Unix-like filesystem and the source control vane. While Hoon itself (`/sys/hoon`) is responsible to

---

[7]Oddly, Perry did not call out weak typing in his enumeration, although he did address it elsewhere in the article.

compile a source noun into a Hoon abstract syntax tree (AST) and ultimately into executable Nock, the actual construction of source input from files is delegated to the `++ford` arm of Clay. This build process includes compiling the correct import files (such as libraries and shared structure files). Clay is also tightly coupled to the userspace vane Gall since system updates and agent updates both occur via Clay.[8]

To motivate how Clay functions as a revision control filesystem, we need to briefly examine some major data structures utilized by Clay. At the highest level, files are organized into "desks", described in previous literature as being analogous to Git branches but really more like Git repositories. A desk is a self-contained continuity of files; its state is the result of a history of commits. Desks may not include links to off-desk resources. Each desk must expose a few files at definite paths; primarily `/mar` for the marks used to read the desk contents.[9]

Ultimately, Arvo and Clay deal in nouns. A noun is a binary tree of unsigned integers. These may be evaluated as Nock formulas or manipulated as data. A noun is formally agnostic to the underlying hardware and is almost always accessed via some representation path (i. e. as phenomenon). A noun serves as a universally legible intermediate representation for all data and code.

Urbit has an immutable data model; the system state of Arvo is the unique result of the events in its history, stored as its event log. If a noun changes, it is the result of definite discrete changes to the system state. This yields very nice properties of referential transparency and has some ramifications in library management; see ~rovnys-ricfer and ~wicdev-wisryt (2024) for more details.

Typically, a noun is altered either directly via subject-modifying code (`%~` censig, `=.` tisdot) or via a mark transformation, on which more later.

---

[8] We omit discussion of several other notable properties of Clay as a single-level store: referential transparency, global addressability, and event-level persistence, for instance.

[9] While Arvo, the vanes, and userspace tools look at other definite locations, in principle one could construct a desk of arbitrary URL-safe paths as long as they are legible to Clay's build process via `/mar`.

While conventional file systems denote file type primarily by file suffix or a cursory search using "magic tests" on the file header, Urbit instead stores all data as a noun accessed via a mark. A mark is essentially a representation rule for nouns. Marks permit nouns to be stored with more granularity than the text/binary dichotomy facilitates, since details of conversion are stored as part of the mark.

A mark may be considered an executable MIME type.[10] A mark essentially describes how to map a data representation to a noun, and from a noun back out to a data representation. This conversion may be trivial (e. g. the binary storage of an audio file) or sophisticated (from a text stream to a linked-list UTF representation). Data are accessed via a particular mark, and the appropriate conversion routine is invoked.[11] Clay is capable of searching for transition paths between mark representations, and in principle permits conversion between all compatible representations (if there were a path from Markdown `md` to rich text `rtf` to plaintext `txt` in marks, then the conversion is automatically supported by Clay).

> A mark is a term (symbol) which is the Urbit equivalent of a MIME type, if MIME types were names of typed validation functions. (~sorreg-namtyv et al. (2016), p. 51)

Unix filesystem mounting and committing involves synchronizing a desk's state with a Unix logical representation of the files involved. The actual file data are imported as `%mime`-typed nouns and then converted to their target mark as file type.

Each mark defines several standard arms:

1. `++grab` converts from other marks (by arm name) to a given mark.

---

[10] A media type (formerly MIME type) is a tag identifier for the intended data format of a particular data entry. We will use "MIME type" as this terminology remains in common use.

[11] This is commonly used with JSON and the Eyre HTTP server vane, for instance.

2. `++grow` converts from the mark to other marks.

3. `++grad` defines the diffs applicators for the mark.

Marks do not need to be symmetrical or round-trip. A JSON input may yield an equivalent JSON output but altered by structural whitespace. Clay is also proactive in searching for possible mark paths—if an immediate conversion is not available, then a mutually available intermediary form may be used. To implement a custom filetype, all that is required is the production of a suitable mark file. Conversions from the filesystem require at a minimum a MIME mark file, which acts as the global intermediary from the host OS.

3.2   Desks

A desk is a filesystem continuity,[12] and represents the main way that data are synchronized between Urbit instances (ships). The state of a desk is a history of sequential commits, with each commit after the first having at least one parent commit. Desks are often analogized to Git repositories.[13] Each desk must contain sufficient internal data—especially marks—to produce its own code, given Hoon and the standard library (which are always available).

Since Clay is a global filesystem, it has to maintain information about both local and remote desks. A local desk's state maintains information about noun data, build and mark cache state, userspace app state, various policies, and synchronization with the host OS filesystem.

Listing 1: Clay desk types

```
::  Domestic desk state.
+$  dojo
  $:  qyx=cult              ::  subscribers
      dom=dome              ::  desk state
```

---

[12]See ~rovnys-ricfer (2024) in USTJ vol. 1 iss. 1, pp. 1—46, section 2.2 for an exposition of the so-called "theory of a desk".

[13]Although desks are synchronized to the host OS as folders, this is a merely a convention, and other schemes of noun organization could employ other organizational abstractions.

```
      per=regs                      ::  read perms per path
      pew=regs                      ::  write perms per path
      fiz=melt                      ::  state for mega merges
  ==
::  Desk state.
+$  dome
  $:  let=aeon                      ::  top id
      hit=(map aeon tako)           ::  versions by id
      lab=(map @tas aeon)           ::  labels
      tom=(map tako norm)           ::  tomb policies
      nor=norm                      ::  default policy
      mim=(map path mime)           ::  mime cache
      fod=flue                      ::  ford cache
      wic=(map weft yoki)           ::  commit-in-waiting
      liv=zest                      ::  running agents
      ren=rein                      ::  force agents on/off
  ==
::  Support types
+$  mizu  [p=@u q=(map @ud tako) r=rang]
                                    ::  new state
+$  rang                            ::  repository
  $+  rang
  $:  hut=(map tako yaki)           ::  changes
      lat=(map lobe page)           ::  data
  ==
```

The keystone structure is hit, which connects a given version of the desk (its aeon, which is merely a @ud) to the tree of associated commits. These are accessed from the "slush pool" of known commits via hut in the Clay's rang, which is not associated with a particular local desk.

Much of Clay's machinery is intended to support noun changes propagated as commits, or desk changes. These may arise from three sources: a local host OS filesystem sync, a remote desk sync, or an on-Urbit local edit. A commit is a snapshot of a set of files with a list of parent commits and a timestamp.

Various merge strategies are available to support desk updating. Given a commit as a timestamped snapshot of files, how should two conflicting histories be reconciled? For instance, %fine is a Git-style "fast-forward" for use when histories nest but one is "ahead". %meet combines changes as long as the same file/noun has not been modified. (Several others are available and are described in the system documentation.) While Clay has at times supported noun diffs in commits, it currently simply stores the entire file at each commit.[14] Urbit developers in practice have not encountered difficulties with desk and commit management due to this limitation at the current time, but resolution using mark diffs will eventually be desirable.

Structurally, Clay tracks desk state as a sequential +$aeon or @ud, but files may be arbitrarily accessed using a +$case:

```
+$    case
  $%    [%da p=@da]           ::    %da:   date
        [%tas p=@tas]         ::    %tas:  label
        [%ud p=@ud]           ::    %ud:   sequence
        [%uv p=@uv]           ::    %uv:   hash

  ==
```

A case resolves into the corresponding aeon via the canonical timestamp of the commit; the label map; or the hash of the corresponding commit. A userspace system to support detailed commit messages, called Story, is available at @urbit/story.

3.3 Runtime

As a vane of Arvo, Clay lives "on Mars"; that is, it describes a logical filesystem inside of the Urbit ship but does not directly map its nouns to physical hardware. The particular implementation used to store the total state of Arvo, which contains Clay's state including file data, depends on the runtime. At the time of writing, the Vere runtime uses the Lightning Memory-Mapped Database Manager (LMDB) which is a B-tree representation for a key-value store (Chu, 2011). While of practical consequence for lookup time and system behavior, the architecture of Clay to an Urbit developer is independent of the runtime implementation.

---

[14]No technical limitation is in place; this was merely a simplification while Urbit data storage is relatively small, and it is expected to be reverted as larger loom sizes—and thus larger nouns—are supported.

The POSIX-compliant host OS supports a filesystem mirror of Clay files organized by desk. Importantly, while these files can be synced to Clay, they are not the canonical reference for each (which lives in LMBD). Clay maintains a "sync duct" with the runtime, which upon receipt of a `%dirk` task produces a list of file changes each way and implements the latest changes.[15]

In principle, as we have intimated, an RCS may abstract away from the file as the fundamental artifact being tracked. While Clay does not fully commit to this, in a concession to its POSIX-compliant host OS, it gestures towards the possibility of conceiving of build sources and artifacts as objects (nouns) other than files. Since Urbit "unifies" nouns (that is, it structurally stores only one copy of a noun and maintains references to that shared value), repetition of critical resources across desks does not lead to filesystem bloat. (See `~rovnys-ricfer` and `~wicdev-wisryt` (2024) in USTJ vol. 1 iss. 1, pp. 75–82, for details.)

3.4   Building Code

Clay is also directly responsible for building code. Formerly, Urbit built code from source files using the Ford vane. In 2020, the core developers realized that integrating the build system directly into the RCS solved a number of problems with updating the system correctly. Updates to the system should be atomic (complete or fail in one transaction); self-contained (no implicit dependencies or dependencies on previous system states); and ordered (sequenced within the system stack). By coupling the build system into the RCS, the system can be updated in a single transaction, with the build system ensuring that the system is always in a consistent state. In a typed RCS, the compiler or build system must be always at hand to process diffs in artifacts. Although of relatively minor consequence to userspace application developers, the integration of `++ford` into Clay transforms the system closer into an integrated RCS for generic nouns.

---

[15]The relevant code is in @urbit/vere at `/vere/io/unix.c`.

3.5 Shortcomings

As currently implemented, Clay presents several wrinkles in developer ergonomics. Chief among these is the way that marks, as simple type tags, are underspecified. The original philosophy of marks centered on network transmission of nouns as tagged data:

> Like a MIME type, the mark is just a label. There is no way to guarantee that the sender and receiver agree on what this label means. A noun which doesn't normalize to itself is a packet drop.
> (~sorreg-namtyv et al. (2016), pp. 51–52)

In practice, different Clay desks and different Urbit versions can have different mark processors (and thus different behvaior for the same tag). No simple version system tracks these; there is no global type registry (other than the scry namespace), and any given mark is simply identified by its desk and path. Developers have expressed a desire for a more robust mark management capability, and solutions have ranged from a global type registry (e. g. that proposed by Archetype) to using paths instead of simple tags for marks. In practice as of writing, marks are disambiguated by supplying the intended mark with the desk; this may lead to multiple different implementations of a mark being present on the same system, although uniquely identified by different Clay paths.

The current architecture of Clay (largely in place by 2016 except for the unification of the former Ford vane into Clay in 2020) leads to three ongoing developer concerns:[16]

1. Implementing RCS behavior at the file system layer seems to be incorrect for Urbit (that is, too much of a sop to Unix). trying to do revision control at base layer, but file system is wrong layer (you just want history of actions/tx log rather than full state); see migrev codebases for clay state

---

[16]This section benefited from discussion with ~tiller-tolbus about the upcoming "shrubbery" project to rework Urbit's userspace.

2. Desks seem to be the wrong abstraction in practice. The theory of the desk doesn't account for actual distribution patterns people would like to use; we want one desk but one spot in file tree is capable of acting as a desk (chroot analysis); overuse of desks makes Urbit not feel as much like a filesystem you can explore

3. The application system (userspace) and the build system and filesystem should be co-located. Currently, Clay and Gall are deeply entangled but must interact via a somewhat awkward message-passing interface. This leads to a number of ergonomic issues, such as the need to suspend a desk in order to suspend an agent. Employing paths rather than simple tags would lead to a desire to constrain what can exist at certain paths. This relates to the definition of files as data structures, and ultimately a noun-maximalist scenario abstracts more towards nouns as database entries rather than "files".

One possible future for Clay sees it being restricted to source and build management, rather than expansion to a more fully-featured filesystem. In this contingency, the userspace management vane may take over conventional file storage, as Gall or a successor. This may only implement a filesystem interface for the host OS and external applications that "think" in files, such as web browsers.

Alternatively, the build system, RCS, and application engine fuse into a single userspace vane, which is a possible endpoint of the "shrubbery" project. Mark cores would be replaced with simpler conversion rules permitting only straightforward type casts between nouns as `$-(from to)` gates.[17]

---

[17]At least two previous models integrating the application layer with the filesystem and build system have been proposed: Hume and the insect model. The insect model in particular surfaced the very Martian concept that "an agent and a document are the same thing."

4 Conclusion

In its current instantiation, Clay exhibits some notable characteristics as a typed revision control system. It is capable of tracking file changes at a structural level, permitting meaningful diffs and merges for files of the same mark. It is also capable of converting between marks, permitting a more flexible approach to file type than the conventional text/binary dichotomy of Git and other RCSs. However, the future of userspace and code building is still in flux and may see a reworking of the Clay vane to better suit the needs of developers and users.⧖

References

Baer, Eric (2018). *What React Is and Why It Matters*. Sebastopol, CA: O'Reilly Media. URL: https://www.oreilly.com/library/view/what-react-is/9781491996744/ch01.html (visited on ~2024.8.12).

Ball, Thomas et al. (2015). "Beyond Open Source: The TouchDevelop Cloud-based Integrated Development Environment." In: *2nd ACM International Conference on Mobile Software Engineering and Systems*. URL: https://ieeexplore.ieee.org/document/7283033 (visited on ~2024.8.12).

Chu, Howard (2011) "LMDB". URL: http://www.lmdb.tech/doc/ (visited on ~2024.8.12).

Collins-Sussman, Ben, Brian W. Fitzpatrick, and C. Michael Pilato (2016). *Version Control with Subversion*. Sebastopol, CA: O'Reilly Media. URL: https://svnbook.red-bean.com/en/1.8/svn.forcvs.binary-and-trans.html (visited on ~2024.8.12).

Hunt, James W. and M. Douglas McIlroy (1976). *An Algorithm for Differential File Comparison*. Computing Science Technical Report 41. Bell Laboratories. URL: http://www.cs.dartmouth.edu/~doug/diff.pdf (visited on ~2024.8.12).

A Note on Subsecond
Base-2 Time Intervals

N. E. Davis ~`lagrev-nocfep`
Urbit Foundation

Abstract

Urbit time provides for the representation of subsecond values down to 2^{-64} s. Such a base-two numbering system prompts the consideration of prefixes for subsecond intervals that are analogous to the IEC 80000-13 prefixes for positive powers of two, as used in memory sizes. We propose a set of prefixes for subsecond intervals that are similar to the SI prefixes for negative powers of ten, and we suggest that these prefixes be used in Urbit time representations. We also discuss the relative error in these prefixes compared to the corresponding negative powers of ten.

Urbit time is conventionally a 128-bit atom,[1] with the lower 64 bits denoting fractions of a second and the upper 64 bits denoting multiples of a second. (That is, 1 s = (`bex 64`).)

By expanding the atomic form of time (`@dr`) to the tuple form, we can clearly see how each component of the time is represented:

```
> (yell now)   :: Treating "now" as an interval.
[d=106.751.991.823.894 h=15 m=19 s=22 f=~[0xd43]]
```

---

[1] Time can actually be an arbitrarily sized atom, but 2^{64} s $\approx 58 \times 10^9$ a; most discussions of noncosmological time will not involve such large intervals.

Urbit Systems Technical Journal I:2 (2024): 51–53.
Address author correspondence to ~lagrev-nocfep.

The last component of the tuple is a list of subsecond time intervals; while `now` does not feign to provide more accuracy than 2^{-16} s, the underlying representation can provide for subsecond intervals down to 2^{-64} s by including more values in the `f` list.

```
> (yell `@dr`0x1)
[d=0 h=0 m=0 s=0 f=~[0x0 0x0 0x0 0x1]]
```

Subsecond decimal time does not cleanly map to this representation, and the resulting hexadecimal values are largely opaque to human interpretation:

Interval	Decimal Value	Hexadecimal Value
1 ms	10^{-3} s	0x41.8937.4bc6.a7ef
1 µs	10^{-6} s	0x10c6.f7a0.b5ed
1 ns	10^{-9} s	0x4.4b82.fa09
1 ps	10^{-12} s	0x119.7998
1 fs	10^{-15} s	0x480e
1 as	10^{-18} s	0x12

Smaller intervals of a second than 2^{-64} cannot be represented in native Urbit time relative time `@dr`.

Urbit time can therefore be more exactly expressed in terms of binary fractions of a second rather than decimal fractions of a second. However, while IEC 80000-13 codified expressions for powers of two that are close to positive powers of ten, there are no expressions for powers of two close to negative powers of ten. We would like to introduce such a scheme for convenience in Urbit time.

Binary Value	Hexadecimal Value
2^{-10} s	0x40.0000.0000.0000
2^{-20} s	0x10.0000.0000.0000
2^{-30} s	0x4.0000.0000
2^{-40} s	0x100.0000
2^{-50} s	0x4000
2^{-60} s	0x10

What prefixes should we provide? The standard names for the positive powers of two that correspond to powers of ten are:

Binary Value	Prefix	Approximation
2^{10}	kibi	10^3
2^{20}	mebi	10^6
2^{30}	gibi	10^9
2^{40}	tebi	10^{12}
2^{50}	pebi	10^{15}
2^{60}	exbi	10^{18}

This suggests that we should prefer prefixes that are similar to the standard names for the negative values of two but with a different last syllable. Following a suggestion by ~rovyns-ricfer for "-ki-", we propose the following prefixes:

Binary Value	Prefix	Symbol	Approximation
2^{-10}	miki	mi	10^{-3}
2^{-20}	muki	μi or ui	10^{-6}
2^{-30}	naki	ni	10^{-9}
2^{-40}	piki	pi	10^{-12}
2^{-50}	feki	fi	10^{-15}
2^{-60}	akki	ai	10^{-18}

As occurs with memory values denominated in kibi, mebi, gibi, etc., it will be important to keep in mind the relative error in such time expressions. We can compare these binary magnitudes roughly to decimal magnitudes and calculate the resulting error, much as we do with the SI prefixes for positive values of ten and two:

Binary Value	Prefix	Approximation	Error
2^{-10}	miki	10^{-3}	2.4%
2^{-20}	muki	10^{-6}	4.9%
2^{-30}	naki	10^{-9}	7.4%
2^{-40}	piki	10^{-12}	9.9%
2^{-50}	feki	10^{-15}	12.6%
2^{-60}	akki	10^{-18}	12.5%[2]

We trust that the current ability to express subsecond intervals in Urbit time will continue to prove useful, and furthermore that the proposed prefixes will promote legibility and accuracy. ❧

---

[2]This is due to truncation error; it "should" be 15%.

Trusting Trust on Mars:
Thoughts on Urbit Security

N. E. Davis ~lagrev-nocfep
Urbit Foundation

Abstract

Via Ken Thompson's classic reflections on compiler
safety and the injection of "undetectable" and irreversible
malicious bugs into binaries, we analyze aspects of the
security of Urbit as a two-level executable system, i. e.
as a virtualized machine running on an execution layer.

Contents

Urbit Systems Technical Journal I:2 (2024): 55–65.
Address author correspondence to ~lagrev-nocfep.

1   Introduction

Ken Thompson's famous 1983 Turing Award lecture, "Reflections on Trusting Trust" (Thompson, 1984), concisely illustrated a fundamental difficulty with reposing confidence in any software stack one has not built oneself from assembler code. He postulated a compiler which had been modified to match a particular pattern and inject malicious code (such as a login backdoor or privilege escalation) into any program it produced; and a more insidious scenario in which the compiler knows to change its own source upon compilation to perpetuate the backdoor attack forwards. His exposition proceeded from the production of a quine, to a learning compiler, to the malicious "trusting trust" attack. The (non)solution Thompson proposed as epitome, "you can't trust code that you did not totally create yourself," was cold comfort to the computer security expert.[1]

Each component of the trusting trust attack can be demonstrated in Nock or Hoon and to some extent realized in Arvo. Countermeasures and implications for the overall security of the Urbit stack are also considered.

2   Nock Quines

A quine is an example of a code program that produces its own source; it is a fixed point of its syntax and execution. Some languages make this relatively straightforward, particularly those with rich string syntax. As Wikipedia states, "quines are possible in any Turing-complete programming language, as a direct consequence of Kleene's recursion theorem"; an older version of the same page emphasizes the utility of the ability to output a computable string.

Nock operates by applying a formula against a subject. The subject–formula pair is reduced by the first matching pattern from the left. A strict quine has no input, however, for Nock

---

[1]Indeed, Forth has been employed as a clean bootstrap platform since it can be implemented straightforwardly in machine language on many target embedded architectures. This is more for pragmatism than security, but the possibility of employing this as a strict security measure exists.

a formula is a partial function that must be evaluated against a subject. We must reconcile the subject as a context but not an input, as it were. A proper Nock quine therefore includes both, and replication of the subject–formula pair should be a requirement for a true quine.

The trivial Nock quine is simply an address replication using the Nock o operator.[2]

```
[[0 1] 0 1] [[0 1] 0 1]
```

Indeed, this suggests a family of quines built on tree structure replication; ~pinhul-radlyr suggested the following:[3]

```
[[[0 1] [[0 2] [0 3]]] [[0 1] [[0 2] [0 3]]]]
```

and the recursive generalization is straightforward. Following Thompson, we consider such a quine to be a "compiler" in that it produces a program from a program.[4]

3   A Learning Compiler

Thompson proceeds from the notion of a quine to constructing a learning compiler, or a compiler that can modify the source of its successor in such a way as to extend the semantics of the language.

Although raw Nock is extremely uncommon in practice on Urbit, it is slightly more common to manipulate vase-mode values of Hoon and rather frequent to modify the Hoon compiler itself (at least in kernel development). A modified Hoon compiler (let us call it "+(Hoon)") is capable of perpetuating language changes forward into the nouns resulting from source. A simple example is adding an additional rune or altering the behavior of the parser (in ++vast) or AST Nock compiler (in ++mint:ut). Given access to one's %base desk, the possible modifications are endless (Listing 1).

---

[2]I am indebted to ~dozreg-toplud for first bringing this simple quine to my attention.

[3]https://github.com/jpt4/icfp2024code/blob/main/quine.rkt

[4]Further articles of interest on producing quines have been provided by David Madore and Eric Hokanson.

Listing 1: A simple example of pattern-detecting adaptive code in Hoon and Nock.

```
::   Hoon
?:(=(- [2 3 4]) [2 3 5] -)
::   Nock
[6 [5 [0 2] 1 2 3 4] [1 2 3 5] 0 2]
```

Given control of a compiler, Thompson then proceeds to spring the trap: "a simple modification to the compiler that will deliberately miscompile source whenever a particular pattern is matched" (p. 763). That is, all code descended from the compromised compiler in his example may be considered contaminated by a self-perpetuating Trojan horse.

Urbit does not directly distribute Nock code as executable nouns today. Any practical attacks based on Nock would require distributing the malicious Nock code as data or inducing a Hoon compiler to produce the malicious Nock code inadvertently. Such compromised code would then have to executed against an appropriate subject to produce the desired malicious consequence.[5]

Critically for Urbit, the Hoon compiler at any one state of the kernel is used to produce the next state. "Live" code is not sent over the network: one sends source files which are then compiled locally into executable Nock nouns. Given such a compromised compiler, "no amount of source-level verification or scrutiny will protect you from using untrusted code" (*ibid.*). The trusting trust attack is complete and the system has been fundamentally compromised.

Another relatively unexplored avenue is to have Nock formula manipulate the rules themselves. Typically, Nock rules are treated as constants, and Hoon code that utilizes them often simply specifies them as such for legibility. This is not necessary, however, and changing the rules this way is straightforward in raw Nock, if a little difficult to conceptualize (a Hoon

---

[5]Since a Nock formula is a partial function, Hoon should be considered as a hypotactic language. That is, each expression is a phrase subordinated to its subject. Crossover manipulations between the subject and formula are thus possible, as long as an iterated cycle of using a formula against a subject to produce a new subject is followed.

example is provided in Listing 2). (This is salient in iterated cycles, a subject–formula pair yielding the next subject for subsequent formula evaluation.)

Listing 2: Hoon which can modify the rules of supplied Nock formulae arbitrarily. For simplicity, lists are used when in practice it would be done in cells and tuples.

```
=/  a=(list @)  [4 1 1 ~]
=|  b=(list @)
|-  ?~  a  (flop b)
$(a t.a, b [?:(=(4 i.a) 3 i.a) b])
```

4   Attacks in Urbit

Nock and Hoon are homoiconic: code and data share the same representation. This facilitates code distribution over Urbit's Ames network, wherein code is transmitted as a raw jammed noun (nominally in Hoon) and then built using local mark conversion, parsing, and compiler routines. The local ship controls its own build process rather than accepting unknown Nock nouns, permitting the source code to be inspected (often in abbreviated form by comparing "desk hashes" or hashes of the contents of a distributed branch) prior to installation.[6] This suggests at least three different programmatic attack vectors for an Urbit ship:

1. Malicious source.

2. False signatures.

3. Compromised compiler.

Each of these could be perpetrated by the last two: the idea of a compromised compiler trumps all bets for a program, and thus prompted Thompson's initial reflections.

---

[6]In practice, we observe that the relatively high trust of the Urbit community has led to the hash being used as a version identifier rather than a cursory security check.

4.1 Malicious source

The most straightforward way to compromise a system is to simply send code that compromises a system in a particular way and induce the target to execute that code. As Urbit code distribution is permissionless, the practical barriers to this are social and habitual: most users prefer to treat the Urbit network as a high-trust society, and most users do not store high-value data (such as wallet keys) on their Urbit ship. However, by representing code as valid, an attacker can execute at least on zero-day exploit against a target.

Furthermore, userspace code distribution does not have permission to modify the %base desk on which the kernel resides. Permission elevation would not be necessary for an attack, however; malicious code could sidestep the per-desk sandbox mechanism by simply directly issuing cards to Clay to modify %base's /sys files.[7] Such would be easy to identify in program source, but would require some diligence on the part of users to hedge against.

Using a social trust mechanism to convince a user to utilize a bad |ota source is by far the simplest mechanism, however.

4.2 Signature falsification

A noun hash is a cryptographic hash of a noun. Specifically, the SHA-256 ++shax of an atom is typically used, or for cell structures the noun is first ++jammed into an atom before a SHA-128 ++shaf is applied. Noun hashes are used extensively in Arvo and the vanes to identify values in caches and to compare nouns for equality.

In principle, signature falsification could lead to invalid cache retrievals, e. g. invoking a malicious gate instead of the intended one. In practice, userspace code does not have any direct access to the Arvo caches, meaning that while signatures

---

[7]At the time of writing, ~hastuc-dibtux pointed out that the %hood agent itself can be used to directly rewire the source. More aggressive countermeasures and a permissioning system will be necessary as Urbit hardens its security model.

could be falsified, this would require a kernel-level or runtime-level compromise of the system.

Ames packet signature falsification   Over the wire, there are two significant kinds of risky false signatures: signed Ames packet or faked desks. An Ames communication takes place as a message is decomposed into 1 kB or smaller packets, each of which is sequentially numbered and signed. All packets are signed using SHA-256 encryption.[8] On the other end, the packets are received in a queue before being reassembled into the original message. We consider three different signature attacks:

1. Falsifying a packet signature. To simply falsify a signature, one would have to falsify the private key of the sender, which is a significant cryptographic challenge.

2. Spoofing a packet signature. A locally compromised runtime could inject a spurious packet matching some hypothetical external ship. This attack is of commensurate difficulty to a simply falsified signature.

3. Permitting a false signature. A compromised Ames vane could maliciously permit a message with a false signature, perhaps activated by the signature itself. This scenario seems the most tractable for a hacker to exploit.

In practice, packet reassembly takes place in the runtime, which introduces another attack surface for these Ames packet signature falsification attacks.

Desk (Clay) signature falsification   A desk hash, used as an informal check,[9] is a signature from the contents of the desk.

We may dismiss the problem of directly producing a malicious source desk that hashes to the same value as a highly nontrivial expenditure of compute resources. In addition, should such an attack come into currency, the hash algorithm could

---

[8]"Every packet sent between ships is encrypted except for self-signed attestation packets from 128-bit comets" ("Ames Overview").

[9]`(shax (jam +<))`, where the referent is a list of commits.

easily be traded for a more complicated and secure one. For a zero-day exploit utilizing the distribution of a compromised desk, prior art suggests that on the order of $2^{63.1}$ SHA operations would be required to construct a collision (Stevens et al., 2017). (Successfully execution would then require that the malicious desk actually contains malicious code, which further complicates the problem space.)

As with the Ames packet signature falsification, it is more likely for malicious desk distribution to succeed via a special-cased desk than by a hash collission. This has an inception problem, of course, since the `%base` desk must be likewise modified (or the threshold attack described below used).

4.3   Compromised compiler

As with pattern-matching examples in the exposition, simple or complex pattern-matching to inject and perpetuate malicious code is a possibility given a Turing-complete language and execution platform. Hoon is of course no exception, so a compromised compiler may alter any outer cores in the current system state and any future nouns produced by the suspected compiler.

Source is of course amenable to inspection, but the trusting trust attack is complete once the compiler is compromised. Thus a compromised compiler is a local problem more than a network-wide risk. The most sensible detection mechanism is to continue rigorous use of hashes to identify nouns and their source uniquely.

5   Attacks in the Runtime

The runtime operates as the computation substrate for Arvo and could execute arbitrary malicious code if compromised. Nock is an interpreted language which is evaluated on some particular virtual machine layer. As of this writing, there are many Nock interpreters **Nock2023** but only two fully instrumented Nock runtimes, Vere and Sword (née Ares). Vere is written in C and utilizes a few third-party libraries statically linked into the binary, such as `libuv`. Sword is composed in Rust and similarly statically links its modules. Per the concerns raised by Thompson about a program produced by a compromised compiler, the runtime could in principle be modified to run malicious code either independently of the Arvo instance or in response to side effects induced by the Arvo instance.

The colloquial wisdom among the Urbit developer community is that if one loses administrative control of one's box (the machine executing the Urbit process), one is already pwned.[10] This is saliently illustrated by the Trusting Trust compiler issue, but of course there are less subtle and more

By inducing a user to install a compromised Urbit runtime, an attacker can achieve full control over a user's ship and its computation, perhaps without the user being aware. Three major components of the runtime could be used to compromise an Arvo instance:

1. Nock evaluation.

2. Cache poisoning.

3. Hint pollution.

Nock evaluation. Nock evaluation in the runtime takes place as some form of bytecode evaluation, rather than evaluating the pure Nock formula. (Subject-knowledge analysis (SKA) further complicates the relationship of on-chip evaluation to the source Nock.) Nock evaluation could be matched for specific patterns and malicious code executed, or simply

Cache poisoning. Like Arvo, the runtime uses caches and the event log extensively to hasten referentially transparent evaluation. We consider two examples, of many possibilities, in which cache poisoning could be used to compromise an Arvo instance.

The first is to compromise the jet state in event playback. (This is a form of "hint pollution.") Jets formally do "nothing" in

---

[10] A related problem is that of the security of Azimuth as a public key infrastructure, but we do not address this line of enquiry in this treatment.

Arvo and are used as a way of creating impure side effects for the Arvo operating function. A compromised jet hint would be a Turing-complete compromise, and incorrect matching of an event playback could result in any possible side effect which the runtime can achieve on the host OS. The user may not be aware of any malicious code execution. Furthermore, due to the way that Vere's jet dashboard matches code, a registered noun can have its associated jet hint removed in the Hoon source but still be invoked due to noun matching; this is a leaky convention that could lead to jet pollution.

The second is to simply poison known caches such as the remote scry cache. Malicious code could thus be emitted to a subscriber *without the host even being aware of the poisoned cache value.* Another upcoming cache susceptible to poisoning is the fastboot cache used to supply compiled nouns in the process of bootstrapping a new ship. Finally, as explicit caching in Arvo is gradually replace with persistent memoization in the runtime, the runtime and its distribution mechanism will need to be provisioned with security assurances for users.

Hint pollution. There is a particular threshold attack which we must consider in detail: the injection of a Nock Eleven flag (with no Hoon side effects, rather evocative of C `#pragmas` but not the same) that nevertheless triggers malicious code execution or exfiltration of sensitive information from the running Arvo instance. A hint is a noun that is used to guide the evaluation of a Nock formula. The compromise can be in the runtime but the trigger in this case comes from the Arvo side.

The most salient attack vector on an Urbit ship, of course, is to compromise the cryptography: emit the Azimuth private key or enough information for an observer to deduce the key. Several of the foregoing techniques, jointly or separately, could be used to achieve this.

In general, of course, the solution is to be paranoid about one's runtime and one's Arvo; if either is discovered to be compromised, it is high time to replace the one and breach the other.

6 Conclusion

As Urbit moves towards automated update processes, such as acquiring and booting into new runtimes directly, secure control over the stack—including the build—will assume new prominence. We hope these reflections will spur more careful consideration of the dangers inherent in running and securing not only Urbit but in fact any computing stack. Fortunately, even at the current time aggressive checking of Urbit (including building one's own runtime binary and checking various hashes proactively) can and should make the likelihood of a trusting trust attack as low as possible, since each check in the process makes it increasingly more difficult to propagate malicious code from previous steps correctly. Such affordances should be propagated into the end-user experience as soon as feasible.▨

References

Stevens, Marc et al. (2017). *The First Collision for Full SHA-1*. Tech. rep. Google Research. URL: https://web.archive.org/web/20180515222208/http://shattered.io/static/shattered.pdf (visited on ~2024.8.12).

Thompson, Ken (1984). "Reflections on Trusting Trust." In: *Communications of the ACM* 27.8, pp. 761–763. DOI: 10.1145/358198.358210.

Urbit Networking:
Ad Fontes

Edward Amsden `~ritpub-sipsyl`,
Ted Blackman `~rovyns-ricfer`
Zorp Corp, Urbit Foundation

Abstract

The Ad Fontes proposal was an influential document outlining a vision for how Urbit networking could be made more reliable and solid-state. Its ideas have remained relevant as remote scry, directed messaging, and other developments have advanced the state of the Ames protocol. This presentation of `~ritpub-sipsyl`'s original document and `~rovnys-ricfer`'s response provides a historical perspective on the development of the Urbit networking stack, and is lightly annotated to connect its ideas to current developments. Some technical details as implemented deviate from the proposal and response.

Contents

Urbit Systems Technical Journal I:2 (2024): 67–87.
Address author correspondence to ~ritpub-sipsyl.

1   Ad Fontes

The original Ad Fontes proposal was produced by ~ritpub-sipsyl on ~2022.12.2 and revised through ~2022.12.10.

1.1   In Principio

On Mars, SIN is taken to an extreme. Logically, Urbit is a single broadcast network – a single big Ethernet wire. Everyone sees everyone else's packets. You don't send a packet. You "release" it. As a matter of practical optimization, of course, routing is necessary, but it is opaque to the receiver. If there is a routing envelope, it is stripped before processing.

An easy way to see this is to compare an Urbit packet, or card, to an IP packet. An IP packet has a header, which is visible both to the routing infrastructure and the application stack. The header, of course, contains the infamous source address. Urbit removes not just the source address, but also the rest of the header. An Urbit card is all payload – it has no region seen both by receiver and router. (~sorreg-namtyv, 2010)

In the classical stack, a basic result of protocol design is that you can't have exactly-once message delivery . To put it in the terms ... [of] subsection 3.2: you can't build a bus on a network. With permanent networking between solid-state interpreters, this feature is straightforward. Why? Because two uniformly persistent nodes can maintain a permanent session

Arvo defines a typed, global, referentially transparent namespace with the Ames network identity at the root of the path. User-level code has an extended Nock operator that dereferences this namespace and blocks until results are available. So the Hoon programmer can use any data in the Urbit universe as a typed constant. (~sorreg-namtyv et al., 2016)

1.2   Nunc

Today there is Ames. Ames provides a command protocol with exactly-once semantics over the wire. Urbit ships can poke other ships and expect eventually once, and only once, action on the poke provided that at some point in the future both hosts are able to communicate. Urbit ships can also watch a path (wire) on another ship and receive updates, provided the subscription is not kicked. Both commands and updates must be acknowledged as a core requirement of the protocol.

What does not exist is a viable implementation of the typed, global, referentially transparent namespace. Neither the interface for application writing, nor the implementation of the stack beneath it, support programming by binding paths in a namespace and apprising other ships of such bindings or permitting them to request such bindings.

This document is in aid of the effort to implement such an interface and networking stack.

1.3   Observations

> As a matter of practical optimization, of course, routing is necessary, but it is opaque to the receiver.

This is a massively important observation. Arvo should not "do routing." It should not be aware of sources or destinations. The runtime may route. Hoon code kept up to date by Arvo for the runtime's use may route. Agents may route. Non-Urbit or quasi-Urbit entities on the network may route. Arvo, a kelvin-versioned artifact which must not be subject to the uncertainty of external technical development, must not route.

1.4   The Stack

From ~rovnys-ricfer:

- PKI

- routing and peer discovery

- transport layer (including packetization)

- scry resolution layer

- frontier discovery layer

- command layer

The PKI can be treated for now as a solved problem. Routing and peer discovery must have presently viable implementations, but nothing which is being kelvined should constrain future, more Urbit-maximalist implementations from creation.

Likewise the transport layer. Urbit needs to function both now, over various Ethernets, and millenia from now, over the Third and Most Glorious Quasiluminal Marterran Subspace Transponsive. Packetization is not something that should be kelvin versioned. None of these problems cry out for an immediate solution, though packetization ought not to churn Arvo's event loop.

1.4.1 Scry resolution

The scry resolution layer is where the rubber meets the road. How are paths bound by remote ships resolved to data? The only possible way is for some ship (initially the binding ship, and later possibly other ships and even non-urbit transponders) to communicate the binding. Since bindings are irrevocable, we call a particular binding an "oath" and we say that a ship will "avow" the oath by taking action to inform others of it.

A ship has no possible way to force its runtime to do anything. Everything depends on the runtime's operations on a given and current state of Arvo. (More of the runtime should be written in Hoon, it should be said.) But a ship can advise or insist that the runtime take some action. Oaths are immutable but may be avowed many times.

1.4.2 Frontier discovery

The frontier is, at this point in time, the limit of what is knowable. In general we do not know all that is knowable. Many ships have bound and even avowed oaths which we have not yet heard of, and may never hear of. But we would like to be able to reliably discover what oaths our peers will avow to us.

Unfortunately, there is no way to do this which is optimal for all applications. The search for such a mechanism is at the root of much of the conceptual and design difficulty for Urbit's networking layer.

We want low-latency, push-based subscriptions. We want low load on large publishers. There is a fundamental tension here.

The correct approach is to provide an interface for applications to implement different strategies in this regard. No networked application can demand absolute upper bounds on delivery latency and absolute reliability.

For example: a chat application might work by eagerly broadcasting avowals of new chat messages, and then beaconing out reavowals in the interim between new chat messages on some configurable but acceptable latency interval. Ten, fifteen, or even thirty seconds of time is not a steep penalty to pay for a dropped packet in a chat application. Of course, this penalty is only paid if the entire message is dropped. If we become aware of a message but we are missing some packets for it, we can always request (see below) an immediate re-send.

A media streaming application, whether for one-to-many broadcast or two-way or many-way communication, may never reavow a binding, since a binding which is known late is no longer relevant.

However, there should of course be a way to request a path from a ship. Thinking of this in terms of "which path exactly must I request?" is incorrect. The information being communicated is "I am interested in a (the latest?) path of this form", which information ought to be avowed, as an oath. This permits replication and caching of interest information, and application-specific but still not onerous handling of the problem of a dead or silent interest.

1.4.3   Command layer

The Ames command layer is, from the view of this system, an application, if a very general and ubiquitous one. A poke takes the form of an oath that you wish to poke another ship with some path and data. The command-layer application insists on re-avowing pokes on a decaying schedule until they are acknowledged. Acknowledgement is, yet again, an oath.

1.5   Routing and discovery, revisited

Alright then. Urbit is conceptually a broadcast network, but we necessarily optimize it by routing. So on what basis to we route, and to where?

Routing must be a decision taken on registration of interest. By what policy we determine interest may vary, but it should be informed primarily by avowals of interest by the destination. An exception is commands which should be routed unless disinterest is avowed.

The public Internet is not a broadcast network, and we cannot yet communicate over a global network where Urbit has its own ethertype and its own routers. Thus we must be able to select a set of public IPs to send avowals (our own or others) to.

For this reason, galaxies already live in DNS. Commands and registration of interest should by default be routed to sponsoring galaxies and be shared with other galaxies. Galaxies learn IPs of their sponsored stars by receiving such communication. Perhaps the registeration of interest is re-avowed on a heartbeat. Similarly, stars learn IPs of their planets by receiving registrations of interest. Any retransmitted avowal can have several lanes attached in the packet header (stripped before offering to Arvo) by which the avowing ship can be reached. Commands can be routed to the IP of the commanded ship, if known, its sponsor's IP, if known, or its sponsor's sponsor's IP. More general oaths are checked against registered interest (which may be expired if not re-avowed) and sent along known lanes to interested ships.

(In an Urbit maximalist future, BGP-type protocols between Urbit-aware routers will likely permit link-shaped routing of such avowals as well as sponsorship-shaped routing, which can reasonably exist now.)

Local networks, by contrast, generally permit and even depend on broadcast behavior. The Address Resolution Protocol is fundamental to the operation of local IP subnets over lower-layer networks. A packet is broadcast which requests a MAC address for an IP, and provides a MAC address to reply to. At higher layers this is replicated. Peer discovery for local networks at the OS layer (DHCP, zeroconf networking), shared-hardware layer (printers and screens) and application layer (media) rely on on broadcast announcements which receive addressed replies. Commands and interest registrations could be broadcast on local networks to discover peers either directly, or via Urbit-aware routers.

2   Response

This appendix is a response by ~rovyns-ricfer *to the original document on* ~2022.12.10 *and revised through* ~2023.1.10.

~ritpub-sipsyl wrote up the philosophy for an Urbit networking paradigm that could be used to realize several different dreams:

- universal referential transparency

- transport agnosticism

- global broadcast

- a "narrow waist" that expresses networking in terms of a small number of primitives that compose well

- layering, to reduce the dimensionality of the problem

2.1   Layers

The main layers are:

- PKI

- Transport

- Routing

- Messaging

- Queries

- Frontier

- Commands

2.2 Layer 1: PKI

The PKI establishes identities, keys, and sponsorship information. The PKI is already factored out well into Azimuth. This document does not propose any changes to that.

2.3 Layer 2: Transport

The transport layer is concerned with packetization, transmission control, congestion control, and packet-level authentication. The messaging layer defines the set of messages, i. e. which nouns can be emitted and received by Arvo as semantically meaningful units of information.

All higher layers should be agnostic to the transport layer. This means they can't know anything about the transport layer – things like how a message is broken into packets, how those packets are authenticated, and how congestion control and transmission control are defined.

A user or an application should be able to configure a ship to use multiple transports. A ship could even use different transports for different subtrees of the scry namespace. This configuration can be thought of as a "scry resolution layer" – someone should be able to mirror any part of the Urbit namespace on IPFS, torrents, i2p, Tor, an S3 server, other Urbit ships, or a USB drive, and as long as the requesting ship has the corresponding plugin for that transport protocol, it should be able to access the data.

The default transport layer should be a UDP-based protocol that looks a lot like the current Ames and Fine protocols: 1kB of data per packet, with some kind of packet forgery prevention to protect against denial of service attacks.

One difference between the proposed default transport and Urbit's current packet-level protocol is that the proposd transport will include "advisory" packets, i. e. packets whose emission does not imply its sender Arvo knows the packet was sent. Advisory acks could be used to indicate that the receiving Vere has heard the packet, without implying that its Arvo has heard it – this will enable incoming message fragment packets to be acked immediately without waiting for a disk write. In contrast, message-level acks do imply the receiving Arvo ingested and processed the message.

2.4   Layer 3: Routing

The basic idea of the routing layer is that each ship maintains a set of other ships with whom it's currently trying to interact, and the routing layer attempts to find the most direct connection possible with each of those ships.

Routing can be transport-dependent. The scry configuration system that allows for different transports to be used for different subtrees applies to routing-related requests too.

The default transport will use symmetric routing with keepalives. For each ship that my ship is trying to communicate with, my ship's routing system will send a keepalive packet every 25 seconds. This keepalive request packet will go down the receiving ship's sponsorship hierarchy, and the response packet will retrace the same path through the network in the opposite direction.

If my ship does not receive the keepalive response within a short window of time (perhaps a few seconds), it will send another keepalive, this time through the ship's sponsor's last known location. If that does not yield a prompt response, my ship sends a keepalive to the sponsor's sponsor's last known location, with this chain terminating in the sponsoring galaxy.

Keepalive responses contain a list of transport addresses that can be used to reach the responder ship. This list will generally include addresses of the sponsorship hierarchy, appended by relays later in the response chain.

(Aside: [Do we want] push-based reconnect? or do we not need that explicit query for sponsee address? Implicit is more efficient and maybe simpler.)

Arvo itself will not maintain an up-to-date list of transport-level addresses for each of its peers. Instead, off-loop code (i. e. part of Urbit whose state is not persisted as part of the Arvo core and whose execution does not occur within Arvo's event loop) will be responsible for maintaining those addresses. For sovereignty reasons, it's good for these systems to occasionally inform Arvo of the known direct addresses for other ships, but that can be done every few minuteswithout hitting the event loop on every state update.

2.5   Layer 4: Messaging

The message layer is the "narrow waist" between the different parts of the system. Every message is simply an $oath: a signed pair of [path noun] representing a scry binding – the path is permanently bound to that noun, and the signature attests to this permanence.

An oath is quite general – it could mean many different things. The higher layers of the system build conventions into the namespace for interpreting oaths whose paths fit certain patterns.

2.6   Layer 5: Queries

The query layer establishes a convention for how one scry binding can be interpreted as a request to download the value bound to a different scry path on another ship. This is a "remote scry protocol". The fundamental interaction consists of a subscriber ship emitting an oath representing a scry request for the value at a fully qualified path, then receiving a response oath from another ship that contains the requested scry binding.

2.7   Layer 6: Frontier

The frontier layer extends the query layer to express a request for the latest value at a path – this can't be a fully qualified scry path, since that implies a concrete $case (revision number or date). Instead, the path in such a request has a wildcard character in place of a $case, indicating the request is a %pine, which can be resolved by any binding whose path matches the path in the request.

The ship receiving the %pine will respond with the latest binding it has that matches the request. Note that for ephemerally bound oaths, such as requesting a piece of data from a Gall agent at the latest date, this operation must be atomic. Breaking it up into two requests (the first to retrieve the case, the second to grab the value at the path with that case) will fail unless both requests are performed on the same Arvo state.

A %pine should only be used when the last case is unknown. Otherwise, a request with a concrete case should be used. This increases the degree of effective referential transparency in the networking – since everything is an oath in this system, everything is at least trivially referentially transparent, but it's good for the referential transparency to be pervasive at every layer, rather than merely trivial. Making more of the requests referentially transparent yields a more stable, cacheable, analyzable system.

2.7.1   Layer 6b: Publications

A further layer on top of queries and %pine is publications. A publication is solid-state, meaning it traces a sequence of scry bindings across the namespace, with an incrementing numeric case for each update.

On initial subscription, a subscriber emits a %pine to request the latest rock. Once it has the rock at revision n, it scries for wave $n + 1$ – not as a %pine, but as a scry request.

The publisher responds in one of three ways to this request: with a scry response if it has the data, with a %nigh response if it doesn't have the data yet, or with a %yore response if it deleted the data. A %yore or %nigh response would bind a path including the original path, but the publisher's current dateas the official $case.

If the subscriber hears a scry response, it requests the next wave, n+2. If it hears a %nigh response, it re-sends the request 25 seconds later. This request should be "sticky", so that if the publisher binds the requested path within 25 seconds of hearing the request, it will immediately route the new binding to the subscriber.

If the subscriber hears a %yore response, that means it has fallen behind the publisher, which has deleted the wave it asked for. The subscriber falls back to a %pine for the latest rock, just like in initial subscription.

2.8 Layer 7: Commands

A command consists of an oath broadcasting a command from the emitting ship to another ship, followed by an oath from the other ship broadcasting the ack, which is either empty, indicating the receiver performed the command, or a $tang error message describing why the command was not performed.

Each command is sent on a "flow", identified by a number called a $bone. Within a flow, commands are delivered to the receiving application in order, with exactly-once delivery at the application level unless one of the two ships breaches.

The transport and routing layers need to know this is a command, so that it can be routed to the receiver despite the receiver not having first emitted an interest oath – every ship is considered to have implicitly registered interest in commands to it.

Note that this design would allow commands to use the same encryption scheme as other broadcasts. This would likely mean the kernel would use a cryptographic ratchet to maintain a secure channel between publisher and subscriber, which the publisher would use to send the subscriber the symmetric keys used to encrypt and decrypt various subpaths within the namespace it's publishing. Since commands will just be one kind of scry binding, they could reuse this key distribution system for forward secrecy.

(Aside: Which ratchet makes the most sense – double ratchet?)

This design also suggests that in the default transport, the receiver of the command would be the ship performing congestion control, which is more polite than the present situation, which is the reverse. All large messages will be pulled, rather than pushed, including commands, giving the ship ingesting the data control over how it obtains the data and at what rate. Only the first packet of a command will be pushed, to notify the receiver the command can be pulled.

2.8　Layer 7: Commands

A command consists of an oath broadcasting a command from the emitting ship to another ship, followed by an oath from the other ship broadcasting the ack, which is either empty, indicating the receiver performed the command, or a $tang error message describing why the command was not performed.

Each command is sent on a "flow", identified by a number called a $bone. Within a flow, commands are delivered to the receiving application in order, with exactly-once delivery at the application level unless one of the two ships breaches.

The transport and routing layers need to know this is a command, so that it can be routed to the receiver despite the receiver not having first emitted an interest oath – every ship is considered to have implicitly registered interest in commands to it.

Note that this design would allow commands to use the same encryption scheme as other broadcasts. This would likely mean the kernel would use a cryptographic ratchet to maintain a secure channel between publisher and subscriber, which the publisher would use to send the subscriber the symmetric keys used to encrypt and decrypt various subpaths within the namespace it's publishing. Since commands will just be one kind of scry binding, they could reuse this key distribution system for forward secrecy.

(Aside: Which ratchet makes the most sense – double ratchet?)

This design also suggests that in the default transport, the receiver of the command would be the ship performing congestion control, which is more polite than the present situation, which is the reverse. All large messages will be pulled, rather than pushed, including commands, giving the ship ingesting the data control over how it obtains the data and at what rate. Only the first packet of a command will be pushed, to notify the receiver the command can be pulled.

2.9 Message Protocol – Interest Paths

Paths of a certain format are recognized by Vere as "interest paths", which register interest (or disinterest) in the value bound to another path. These paths all use %a as their $vane, representing the Ames vane.

2.9.1 Request Types ($cares)

- %a: fetch a value at a fully qualified path (remote scry)

- %b: fetch the latest value (%pine)

- %c: send command (%poke)

2.9.2 Response Types

- %d: poke ack

- %z: metadata about whether a path is bound and available

2.9.3 Remote Scry Motif

The remote scry motif implements a remote query at a fully qualified path. It is primarily a request/response system where a request for the value at a path yields a single formal response containing the requested value. This motif also includes advisory responses that the publisher can emit as a courtesy if it is not sending the formal response at this time.

Request

```
path:  /~rovnys/1/2/a/a/~2023.1.10/~zod/2/3/c/x/4
    /base/sys/hoon/hoon
value: &
```

The value bound to a scry request path is a flag indicating interest if yes, or disinterest if no. Disinterest can be used to cancel a previous request.

Positive Response (Permanent, Value is Present)

```
path:   /~zod/2/3/c/x/4/base/sys/hoon/hoon
value: [~ %hoon '::  hoon 141k\0a...']
```

The value in any permanent response is a (unit [mark noun]).

Negative Response (Permanent, Value Is Absent)

```
path:   /~zod/2/3/c/x/4/base/nonexistent/hoon
value: ~
```

A permanent negative response binds the requested path directly to a null value.

Blocked Responses

A blocked response represents a refusal to answer the scry request. Any blocked response binds a temporary path to a value indicating the kind of refusal. The path is bound at the current date with a %z care, and it includes the original scry request path as the spur.

Deleted

This response is emitted if the publisher has deleted the value at this path.

```
path:   /~zod/2/3/a/z/~2023.1.10/~zod/2/3/c/x/4/base
    /sys/hoon/hoon
value: %yore
```

Not Yet Bound

This response is emitted if the publisher knows it might bind the path later, but has not yet bound the path to any value.

This can happen if the subscriber asks for a Clay file or publication data at a future $case.

```
path:  /~zod/2/3/a/z/~2023.1.10/~zod/2/3/c/x/4/base
    /sys/hoon/hoon
value: %nigh
```

General Refusal (Other)

There are other reasons the publisher might not want to respond: for example, the request could be malformed, causing a crash in the scry handler; or the value might not have permissions to be read over the network. This response is a catch-all that does not provide any information about why the request was denied.

```
path:  /~zod/2/3/a/z/~2023.1.10/~zod/2/3/c/x/4/base
    /sys/hoon/hoon
value: %deny
```

2.9.4   Fetch at Latest (%pine) Motif

The %pine motif implements a "query at latest" request/response flow. The requester asks for the latest value at a scry path whose $case (revision number or date) is a wildcard (?). The request has a different $care to indicate it's a %pine rather than a scry request. The publisher responds with a path that matches the request predicate, with the latest response it can, as a direct binding, or a generic blocked response.

Request

```
path:  /~rovnys/1/2/a/b/~2023.1.10/~zod/2/3/c/x/?
    /base/sys/hoon/hoon
value: %ud
```

The value of a %pine request indicates which kind of $case it wants in the response path. A case can be either %ud for

This can happen if the subscriber asks for a Clay file or publication data at a future $case.

```
path:   /~zod/2/3/a/z/~2023.1.10/~zod/2/3/c/x/4/base
    /sys/hoon/hoon
value: %nigh
```

General Refusal (Other)

There are other reasons the publisher might not want to respond: for example, the request could be malformed, causing a crash in the scry handler; or the value might not have permissions to be read over the network. This response is a catch-all that does not provide any information about why the request was denied.

```
path:   /~zod/2/3/a/z/~2023.1.10/~zod/2/3/c/x/4/base
    /sys/hoon/hoon
value: %deny
```

2.9.4   Fetch at Latest (%pine) Motif

The %pine motif implements a "query at latest" request/response flow. The requester asks for the latest value at a scry path whose $case (revision number or date) is a wildcard (?). The request has a different $care to indicate it's a %pine rather than a scry request. The publisher responds with a path that matches the request predicate, with the latest response it can, as a direct binding, or a generic blocked response.

Request

```
path:   /~rovnys/1/2/a/b/~2023.1.10/~zod/2/3/c/x/?
    /base/sys/hoon/hoon
value: %ud
```

The value of a %pine request indicates which kind of $case it wants in the response path. A case can be either %ud for numeric revision, %da for date, %tas for label, or %uw for hash. If the publisher can't bind a path at the requested $case type, it will emit a general refusal block response.

Response

The %pine response message is the same as a scry response message. Its path has a concrete case, not a wildcard.

```
path:  /~zod/2/3/c/x/4/base/sys/hoon/hoon
value: [~ %hoon '::  hoon 141k\0a...']
```

2.9.5   Command (%poke) Motif

Request

```
path:  /~rovnys/1/2/a/c/1.234/~zod/2/3/a/d/1.234
    /~rovnys/36
value: [/g/landscape/chat/my-channel %add-post
    'first!!1']
```

Here 36 is the $bone, i. e. the number of this "flow" between the two ships. 1.234 is the message sequence number, which is also the case of the request path. The poke request can be thought of as expressing interest in the ack message bound by the receiving ship.

Positive Response (Ack)

```
path:  /~zod/2/3/a/d/1.234/~rovnys/36
value: &
```

If the receiver performed the command, it emits a response on the requested ack path with a value of & ("yes").

Negative Response (Nack)

```
path:   /~zod/2/3/a/d/1.234/~rovnys/36
value: [| 'chat %add-post failure:' 'no permissions
    for this channel' ~]
```

If the receiver declined to perform the command, it emits a response on the requested ack path containing a | ("no") and a $tang datum containing either a stack trace or an application-level error message. Note that this is not intended as a general-purpose response mechanism, i. e. it is an anti-pattern to dispatch on the stack trace programmatically.

(Aside: Should there be a way to dispatch on the kind of error? Userspace devs keep asking for this. We could easily make the poke motif a special case of a more general request/response motif. That arguably violates CQRS, but it's a very useful pattern, both for errors and for things like responding to a command with a ticket number that the requester could use later to check in on the status of an ongoing async operation that this command kicked off.)

(Aside: Should there be an explicit disinterest message that can be sent in response to a poke, as an advisory scry binding? This could be useful for mitigating DoS attacks, and it could even specify an explicit backoff interval.)

2.10   Handshake Motif

Any two ships need to able to negotiate a symmetric key to distribute other symmetric keys that will be used to encrypt scry $spurs (the last part of the scry path, after all the standardized path elements) and bound values.

An encrypted spur looks like /14/0w2.CESjp.GdASq. zpdVc.b4Y1T.JXcY1, where 14 is the number of the key used to encrypt the second element of the path, which is the result of jamming (serializing) and then encrypting the original spur. Any of the spurs used as examples of remote scry and %pine in this document could be replaced by a spur of this form without loss of generality. Poke paths are not encrypted, only their values.

(Aside: Should poke values always be `[key-num encrypted-value]` just like encrypted spurs? That might be nice, to avoid race conditions between the handshake protocol and other pokes.)

Since cryptography evolves, it cannot be kelvin versioned. Urbit's handshake protocol should instead have an incrementing version number. As of this writing in 2023, modern protocols use various kinds of "cryptographic ratchet" to cycle keys frequently, providing forward secrecy and sometimes other desirable privacy properties. These ratchets often involve "ephemeral Diffie-Hellman" key exchange and "key derivation functions (KDFs)" to limit how far back or forward an attacker could see if they crack any single key.

The network messages to request a symmetric key used to encrypt scry `$spurs` can use the normal `%pine` and remote scry motifs. The `$spurs` involved in the request itself will be encrypted using the latest key negotiated by the handshake protocol.

Any handshake protocol can be expressed as pokes back and forth between the two ships, encrypted using the latest known key negotiated by the handshake protocol. So that both ships know that a poke relates to a handshake, we could reserve bone `0` for the handshake protocol.

The first implementation of this networking design will likely triage the handshake and use the Diffie–Hellman of both ships' static keys as a permanent symmetric key. This does not provide forward secrecy, but keeping the handshake protocol orthogonal from the rest of this suite of protocols allows a non-trivial handshake protocol to be added later without changing the rest of the design.

2.11 Routing

Note that since routing is transport-dependent, there are no message-level semantics, other than Arvo emitting oaths to its local Vere to indicate interest or disinterest in routing messages to a ship.

Ford Fusion

Ted Blackman ~rovnys-ricfer
Urbit Foundation

Abstract

Ford Fusion was an overhaul of Urbit's over-the-air upgrade process and a rewrite of its build system. The new update system corrected a few long-standing bugs with the previous one, and the new build system is simpler, smaller (by around 5,000 lines), and easier to manage. This historical report was published on the Urbit Blog as a capitulation of the project, which successfully revamped the Hoon code build system. It is lightly annotated to update the minor technical changes that have occurred since the original publication; this is intended as a living document to some extent. Ford Fusion remains the state of the art for building Urbit software as of writing.

Contents

Urbit Systems Technical Journal I:2 (2024): 89–104.
Address author correspondence to ~rovnys-ricfer.

This Ford Fusion description was released by ~rovnys-ricfer *on* ~2020.7.14.

1   Overview and Rationale

Ford Fusion was an overhaul of Urbit's over-the-air upgrade process and a rewrite of its build system. The new update system corrects a few long-standing bugs with the previous one, and the new build system is simpler, smaller (by around 5,000 lines), and easier to manage.

Since deployment of Ford Fusion to the livenet in late June, over-the-air updates (OTAs) have been much smoother. Before Ford Fusion, it was common for an OTA to take several hours, use too much memory, and leave ships in inconsistent states. After Ford Fusion, multiple OTAs have been pushed out, including kernelspace changes, and most users didn't even notice.

Urbit has always been able to update itself OTA, but this process has often been rocky. Updating an operating system kernel on-the-fly is a difficult problem in general, like performing heart replacement surgery on yourself while running a marathon. Code that allows Linux to update its kernel in this way became a startup called Ksplice, won multiple awards, and sold to Oracle. Even that, as impressive as it is, and as brilliant as its programmers are, can only perform certain limited kinds of patches to the kernel.

Urbit isn't exactly a traditional operating system, so the comparison is somewhat unfair, but the purpose of better architecture is to create unfair comparisons. In this case, because the Nock layer is frozen, upgrading everything above that layer is easier. Upgrades are also facilitated by pure-functional semantics, transactional event processing, a type system oriented toward concrete data, and orthogonal persistence. These features make it feasible for Urbit to upgrade itself in the general case, not just some special cases.

Ford Fusion has fixed the major upgrade issues of the past by guaranteeing three properties that in retrospect are obvious requirements, but, like much of Urbit, took many years and rewrites to identify as such:

- Atomic: the update should complete or fail in one transaction. If it fails, the system shouldn't get stuck.

- Self-contained: there must be no implicit dependencies or hysteresis (dependence on previous system states) when building the new software from source.

- Ordered: updates must be monotonically sequenced from the system's lowest layer to highest.

Let's walk through them one by one.

1.1 Atomicity

In previous versions of Urbit, updates failed atomicity by deferring parts of the update to later events, which are separate transactions that can fail independently. Generally, each deferral causes an exponential increase in the number of failure states that needed to be handled.

We've learned that asynchronicity is an entropic state. A system will tend toward more asynchronicity over time unless effort is put into keeping it synchronous. As developer Jonathan Blow has noted (Blow (2019), 42m27s), the language server protocol has turned every editor plugin into a distributed system, since now it has to communicate asynchronously with the main editor process.

Consider an update system that took multiple Arvo events to complete. An ad-hoc higher-level transaction system would need to be built to roll back the effects of the first few events in case of failure. It's important for various parts of the system to be able to emit effects on upgrade; since those effects would need to be rolled back if a later event in this upgrade fails, the system would need to maintain a queue of those events and only apply them once all the other upgrade events have completed.

Note that the asynchronicity has now spread. Some effects that would normally be guaranteed to be processed synchronously might now be asynchronous. Entropy has begun to take hold, chipping away at the set of invariants the system is capable of guaranteeing.

This observation is not purely theoretical. False modularity was the cause of internal asynchronicity in Clay where it had to wait for responses in a complex dance with Ford, which was another vane (Arvo kernel module); moving Ford into Clay allowed function calls that were synchronous from Clay's perspective, which allowed further simplifications, culminating in about a twenty percent reduction of source code size of the Arvo kernelspace.

Steve Yegge's "platform rant" (Yegge, 2011) describes a Bezosian edict prohibiting synchronous communication among modules through direct linking. This can be seen as an acknowledgment of the difficulty Amazon was going to have when it needed to turn internal services external. If your software needs to run in hell, build it that way from the start.

An Urbit ship is not an enterprise SaaS product and does not need to run in this hell; it exists for just one person, with natural pressure pushing it in the opposite direction from Amazon's web services. Instead of needing a ship's state and functionality sharded into microservices strewn across multiple clusters, an Urbit instance is easiest to manage as a single server with all its state unified into one data structure and its event log stored as one totally ordered sequence of state updates – the antithesis of a distributed system.

1.2   Self-Containment

Before Ford Fusion, each commit to the Clay filesystem validated its files using filetypes (called "marks") defined by files in the previous commit (see ~lagrev-nocfep (2024), pp. 35–50 in this issue). This could cause bugs if the filetype definitions had changed in a backward-incompatible manner. It also meant a commit could not add both a new filetype and new files of that type; instead, you needed two commits: one to define the filetypes, and a second to add files of that new type. More theoretically, it caused history-dependence. The validated contents of files in a commit could vary based on the history of commits that led to this one.

Another way source code failed to be self-contained was that it had access to symmetry-breaking information at build-time, namely ship, desk (Urbit's answer to a git branch), and (faked) date. A build recipe should be able to shared, cached, and rerun without dependence on local conditions, so user code now no longer learns its ship, desk, or date until runtime.

Source code also had build-time access to Urbit's immutable global namespace, called the "scry namespace", which the kernel makes available as an implicit argument to userspace Hoon code. The scry namespace is immutable and referentially transparent, i. e. a request must always yield the same result for all time, but if an agent asks the kernel for a resource that's from the future, hosted on another ship, or to which that agent doesn't have permission, the kernel will deny the request.

If the kernel denies a scry request that user code made during the build process, the build system has no choice but to treat it as a nondeterministic error. Nondeterministic errors can never be fully eradicated, if for no other reason than that the user always has the option to defenestrate the machine—there's nothing deterministic about that. But we try to minimize them, and especially to minimize uncertainty as to under what conditions they might occur.

No build should be killed by the absence of files outside the desk, so as of this update, user code can no longer scry at build time. Once built, userspace programs can scry if run in a context with a scry handler; a Gall agent's runtime scry requests still work just fine.

1.3 Order

The final kind of failure fixed by Ford Fusion was the lack of ordered layering during a software update. The most common form of this failure was that old Ford had a tendency to try to build userspace code using the previous version's standard library. This didn't work too well, unsurprisingly.

Emerging from this underworld required making a number of changes to the Arvo kernel, Clay, Gall, and the procedure for kernel updates. To avoid turning into a pillar of salt, I'll skip the details of how the old system worked and instead describe the new update procedure.

2 How Updates Work Now

These are the layers of the stack that update themselves on the fly, from lowest to highest:

1. `/sys/hoon`: the Hoon language definition and compiler

2. `/sys/lull`: common type definitions for Arvo, its vanes, and userspace

3. `/sys/arvo`: the Arvo kernel proper and related type definitions

4. `/sys/zuse`: the standard library

5. Vanes: Arvo kernel modules, including Clay itself

6. Userspace: apps, marks, ancillary source code like libraries, and user data

An update to one layer necessitates a reload of all layers above it; e. g., a change to Zuse should trigger updates to the vanes and userspace. Conversely, an update to a higher layer should not cause a spurious reload of lower layers, which should not be affected by the change; for example, an update to just userspace should not cause any reloads of system code.

Clay is responsible for enforcing the layering of updates. An update to a module is triggered when an attempt is made to commit a change to Clay that affects one or more files needed to build the module. For example, if the `foo` agent's source, defined in `/app/foo/hoon`, imports the `bar` library from `/lib/bar/hoon`, then a modification to `/lib/bar/hoon` triggers an update to the `foo` agent. All vanes and userspace files depend on Zuse, which depends on the Arvo and Hoon sources, so a change to the Hoon, Arvo, or Zuse sources will trigger updates to all vanes and userspace files.

When asked to perform a commit, Clay determines which layers need to be updated based on which files have changed and which modules depend on those files. For now, all running programs load their source from the `%base` desk, so only changes to `%base` trigger stateful updates. Files in other desks can be built, but not installed into the system. This might be relaxed in the future.

The process of updating varies by layer. The Hoon and Zuse layers are stateless, so their newly rebuilt cores (Nock executables) must be stored (somewhere in the system's Nock tree, in memory; remember, Urbit is a single-level store), but they have no state that would need to be migrated. The Arvo kernel, vanes, and userspace agents are all live, stateful programs, so in order to update one of those, the system must extract the state from the old program, pass that data into the newly built program, then discard the old program and store the new one. Arvo and agent state injection routines can emit effects, but vane updates cannot.

To work around this limitation, Gall has a two-phase update process. First it enters a dormant "pupal" phase that stores not running agent cores, but only the agent states that the old Gall had extracted from its agents. When Clay notifies Gall that its agents have been rebuilt, Gall "molts" back into normal functionality by loading the agent cores from Clay and then running their `+on-load` routines to inject the old state.[1]

---

[1] Including agent state upgrade handling.

If there's a change to files in /sys on the %base desk, Clay asks Arvo to update kernelspace. Clay sends a sequence of moves (effects) to Arvo to ask Arvo to perform any necessary updates to Hoon, the kernel, Zuse, and vanes. This sequence is terminated by an extra move back to Clay itself, which will be received by the updated version of Clay after migrating its state. The rebuilt Clay can then use the newly rebuilt version of Zuse to rebuild userspace and notify clients of the update. One client is Gall, which molts when Clay notifies it.

Clay triggers updates, but the Arvo kernel is responsible for performing updates to all kernelspace layers, and Gall is responsible for updating userspace agents. Agents are stored in Gall's state, but all other layers are stored directly in the Arvo core's state, so the Arvo kernel contains the routines that reload Hoon, the kernel itself, Zuse, and the vanes.

The Arvo kernel reloads itself by compiling the future version of itself, then calling the new core's +load routine with the relevant parts of the old state. The state passed to the new Arvo now includes not just the vane cores and their states, but also the Arvo "duct" call stack, which maintains a stack of queues of moves to be passed from one vane to another, and a list of effects to emit to Unix at the end of the current Arvo event. If needed, Arvo could migrate the outstanding moves themselves – if, say, the duct datatype changes.

Passing the Arvo call stack state to new Arvo allows a kernel update to happen in the middle of a more complex event without disturbing other sequences of processing steps happening concurrently in the vanes.

This entire update process happens in one Arvo event and doesn't break event-dispatching semantics. This not only provides atomic rollback, but allows the update to be combined with other actions into a larger transaction – for example, to stage complex changes, user code could trigger two kernel updates in a row, both in the same event.

Note that this is the opposite situation from the entropically leaking asynchronicity described earlier. Now the guarantees don't deteriorate; they can be composed into stronger guarantees.

3   How Clay Validates a Desk

A desk is Urbit's answer to a Git repository. It's almost identical, except all files are typed and validated, and whenever a commit becomes the equivalent of Git's HEAD, it's assigned a semantically meaningful revision number, and all files are typed and validated.

If Clay has been asked to perform a commit, it needs to validate all the files in this desk and notify all subscribers to live queries of this desk's data. Gall, for example, maintains live queries on builds of its live agents. Validation uses the Ford build system, which as of this update is no longer a standalone vane but a core within Clay.

A Clay commit, like a Git commit, is specified as the current value of all its changed files (and, separately, references its parent commits by hash), not as the diff from a parent commit. Unlike Git, Clay is typed, and every file must be validated according to its "mark". A mark is named like a file extension, e.g., %txt, %png, or %noun, and Clay maintains a mapping from that name to behaviors of values of that type under various operations. The last segment of any Clay path specifies the mark to use for operations on that file, including validation.

Mark operations include conversion to and from other marks (such as converting %json to %txt), revision control operations (diff, patch, and merge), and validating an untyped noun. Operations for mark %foo-bar are defined by a core built using the source code at /mar/foo-bar/hoon, or if that doesn't exist, at /mar/foo/bar/hoon.

Consider a file at /web/foo/json. In order to validate this file, Clay must load the mark definition core and use its validation routine to ensure the untyped value of /web/foo/json is in fact valid JSON. To obtain this core, Clay must build the file at /mar/json/hoon from source and then process the resulting raw mark core using some mild metaprogramming to get a standard interface core for dealing with marks, called a $dais, whose type is defined in Zuse.

Since building a source file only makes sense if the file has been validated as a %hoon file, but mark definitions themselves must be built from source, there's a logical dependency cycle – who validates the validators? To break this cycle, Clay hard-codes the validation of %hoon files. This allows mark definitions to be built from source, and in fact any file can depend on any other file of any mark as long as there are no cycles. As of Ford Fusion, Ford performs a cycle check to ensure acyclicity.

Since building a file is a pure function, Clay memoizes the results of all builds, including builds of marks, mark conversions, and Hoon source files. These memoization results are stored along with the desk and are used by later revisions of that desk. Future work should allow merge commits to pull memoized builds from all parents, but for now only the previous revision of the current desk is used. This is a major simplification of previous Ford architectures, which maintained much more complex caches with less clear eviction semantics. Now on every commit, we just throw away any unused memoized builds from the previous revision's Ford cache.

Once Clay has validated every file in this new revision of a desk, it constructs and sends updates to any subscriptions that other vanes or agents have requested. More Ford builds may be run to fulfill these requests, including builds for any running agents whose dependencies changed in this commit.

When Gall receives a newly rebuilt agent from Clay, it calls the gate produced by the +on-load arm of the new agent with the state extracted from the old agent. If there is a crash in any +on-load calls or in the handling of any effects they emit (which can include more agent activations), then the whole event crashes, canceling the commit. This effectively gives any agent the ability to abort a commit by crashing.

It is a bit counterintuitive that an app reload failure could prevent a kernel update. The reason is that we don't want the system to update itself into a broken state. An Urbit can be rendered practically unusable by the presence of broken agents, even if the kernel hasn't lost integrity, so it's kinder to the user not to break their agents by installing an incompatible kernel update. This also puts virtuous pressure on kernel developers not to "break userspace", the importance of which has been insisted on for decades by Linus Torvalds, among others.

If an agent does crash a commit event that included a kernel update, the attempted commit is now trivially rolled back, and the system can deliver an error message to the user. This does not leave the system in an inconsistent or stuck state, so the user could modify the failing agent and try the kernel update again later. Supporting better workflows for keeping third-party agents up-to-date will be an important aspect of Urbit's upcoming software distribution work.

4 Ford Build Semantics

4.1 The Three Types of Ford Builds: Files, Marks, and Casts

The Ford build semantics have been simplified. There are now three kinds of builds that Ford can perform: files, marks, and casts, all of which happen synchronously as function calls inside Clay and are available (without memoization) as scry interfaces.

4.1.1 File Builds

A file build takes in a filepath containing Ford runes and Hoon source, runs the Ford runes to perform imports, and then compiles the source, producing a `$vase`, a noun tagged with its Hoon type.

Clay exposes file builds into the scry namespace with `%ca`: as an example, `.^(vase %ca /~zod/base/3 /lib/sole/hoon)` will build the `sole` library.

4.1.2 Mark Builds

A mark build produces a `$dais` mark-interface core. It first performs a file build on the Hoon file in `/mar` that defines the mark core, then it does some metaprogramming to make the operations more convenient to use. If the raw mark core delegated revision control operations to another mark core, the mark build will also load the delegate mark core and resolve the result into the `$dais`.

Clay exposes mark builds into the scry namespace with
`%cb`: as an example, `.^(dais:clay %cb /~zod/base/3 /mar/foo/hoon)` builds a `$dais` for the `%foo` mark.

4.1.3   Cast Builds

A cast build produces a `$tube`: a gate that takes a value of one
mark as input and converts it to a valid value of another mark
or crashes. To convert from mark `%foo` to mark `%bar`, Clay
tries the following operations, in order:

1. direct grow from '

2. direct grab from '

3. indirect jump from '

4. indirect grab from '

The `%foo` mark can "grow to" `%bar` by providing an arm in
its `+grow` core named `+bar`. `%bar` can convert from `%foo` using
a `+foo` arm in its `+grab` core. `%foo` can also chain a conversion
through an intermediary using an arm in its `+jump` core, and
`%bar` can specify an "indirect grab" by having a `+grab` arm produce a delegate mark instead of directly defining a conversion
gate.

Clay exposes cast builds into the scry namespace with
`%cc`: as an example, `.^(tube:clay %cc /~zod/base/3 /foo/bar)` builds a `$tube` conversion gate from `%foo` to `%bar`.

4.2   Ford Runes

There are now only seven Ford runes. A file can contain zero,
one, or many of each, but each Ford expression can only be one
line, and they must be in the standard order of `/-`s, `/+`s, `/=`s,
and then `/*`s.

```
/-  foo, *bar, baz=qux
```

The `/-` rune imports a structures file from `/sur`. You can
import it as just `foo`, in which case the build result of that file

(usually a core with mold definitions) will be pinned into the compilation subject with the face `foo`. If you prefix it with a `*` as in `*bar`, the result will be pinned into the subject with no face; if the structures file compiled to a core, this exposes all the arms into the namespace of the compilation subject. Finally, if you import it as `baz=qux`, the `baz` face will be applied instead of `qux`. This is similar to "import as" in other languages.

```
/+  foo, *bar, baz=qux
```

The `/+` rune imports a library file from `/lib`. Aside from the different source folder, the syntax and semantics are the same as for `/-`.

```
/=  clay-raw  /sys/vane/clay
```

The `/=` rune imports the result of building a Hoon file from a user-specified path (the second argument), wrapping it in a face specified by the first argument. The final `/hoon` at the end of the path must be omitted. This is mostly useful for importing a file for testing. The file at the specified path will be built as a normal userspace Hoon file; i. e. its compilation subject will be Zuse augmented with the results of any Ford runes it has at the top of the file.

```
/*  hello-gen  %hoon  /gen/hello/hoon
```

The `/*` rune imports the contents of a file in the desk, specified as the third argument with the full path including the trailing mark, converted to the mark specified by the second argument, and pinned into the compilation subject wrapped in the face specified by the first argument. This can be used to import static data at build-time, such as a data file, a media file, or, in the case of this example, a Hoon file as source text rather than already built.

A valid userspace Hoon file must contain a nonempty list of `hoon`s (Hoon source expressions) below the Ford runes, separated by gap (more than one space, or at least one newline). The system wraps this list of `hoon`s in a `=~` expression so that the result of the previous `hoon` is used as the subject of the next `hoon`. The result of the Ford runes is used as the compilation subject for this =~ hoon; informally, the shape of the compilation subject can be thought of as:

```
:*    fastar-2   fastar-1
      fastis-2   fastis-1
      faslus-2   faslus-1
      fashep-2   fashep-1
      <zuse>
==
```

```
/$   some-face   %from-mark   %to-mark
```

The /$ rune imports a mark conversion gate between two types. These are marks on the same desk as the file.

```
/~   some-face   some-type   /some/directory
```

The /~ rune imports, builds, evaluates, and pins the results of many hoon files in a directory. Each Hoon file in the specified directory will be built and evaluated. The result of evaluating each file will be added to a ++map and pinned with the specified face some-face. The keys of the map will be the name of each file, and the values of the map will be the result of evaluating each file and casting its result to the type specified some-type.

All of the hoon files in the specified directory, when evaluated, must produce data of a type that nests under the type specified some-type. File with a mark other than %hoon will be ignored.

```
/%   some-face   %some-mark
```

The /% rune imports a mark definition from the /mar directory. The mark definition will be built and pinned with the specified face some-face.

5   Future Work

Urbit still needs to make better use of desks other than %base and the development process should be adjusted given the tighter coupling between source code and kernel and tighter criteria for accepting an update.

This work also hopefully provides a good foundation of a package management and software distribution system for Urbit. As ~wicdev-wisryt has said, a user should be able to run |install ~norsyr-torryn %canvas to load and build remote source. No one should experience dependency hell on Urbit, but we're not there yet.

At least now, building a desk has no dependencies, other than a Ford with a compatible Hoon compiler. No decisions have been made on this yet, but Ford might get moved to inside the desk, possibly by making Zuse callable. This could allow a desk to expose a Nock interface in addition to a typed Hoon interface, which could even let a desk be used as a "pill" bootloader.

6   Conclusion

~littel-ponnys and I (~rovnys-ricfer) spent most of 2018 rewriting Ford with the intent of improving its performance. Compared to its predecessor, its result was better in some ways but worse in others. The caching system was labyrinthine and poorly factored, making the system difficult to debug or prove correct, even informally. Some things were faster, but the caching and dependency tracking were actually complex enough that a number of common operations, like mark conversion, were too slow.

In early 2020, ~master-morzod suggested moving Ford into Clay to reduce asynchronicity. It seemed absurd at first, but at some point I realized I could combine that idea with a simpler build-caching scheme and self-contained desk builds, and ~wicdev-wisryt realized he could use that to further simplify Clay's commit and merge code, which he did as part of this project.

The first time I rewrote Ford, it took me six months, with help from ~littel-ponnys, and it weighed in at 6,000 lines of code. The second time, in late 2018, took a few weeks. The third time, in January 2020, took a week. I wrote +ford in Ford

Fusion in one long day, and it's about 500 lines of synchronous, functional code.

It has taken me two or three years to understand this problem as well as I do, and I expect there are parts of it I still don't understand. The code itself isn't the issue; it's finding the right answer to ontological and teleological questions. What *is* Ford? What will it be in a hundred years? I'm confident Ford Fusion is more similar than its predecessor to the Ford of 2120, because it's smaller, more functional, and easier to understand and administer.

As an engineering discipline and organizational practice, working on a system intended to be frozen yields surprising simplifications like this every so often. Urbit is now reaching the point where we're starting to see more of the obsidian edges of the frozen future system emerge from the lava.⊚

References

Blow, Jonathan (2019) "Preventing the Collapse of Civilization". URL: https://youtu.be/pW-SOdj4Kkk?t=2547 (visited on ~2024.8.30).

~lagrev-nocfep, N. E. Davis (2024). "Clay as a Typed Revision Control System." In: *Urbit Systems Technical Journal* 1.2, pp. 35–50.

Yegge, Steve (2011) "Stevey's Google Platforms Rant". URL: https://gist.github.com/chitchcock/1281611 (visited on ~2024.8.30).

Eyre HTTP Caching

Mark Staarink ~palfun-foslup,
Ted Blackman ~rovyns-ricfer,
Joe Bryan ~master-morzod
Tlon Corporation, Urbit Foundation, Urbit Foundation

Abstract

Eyre is the server vane for the Urbit OS, and is responsible for handling all HTTP requests. Eyre supports caching responses to GET requests, which can improve performance by reducing the number of times that the server must generate a response from scratch. This historical report and response were published as advisory gists on GitHub, and encapsulate design decisions that have gone into modifying and improving Eyre's caching performance.

Contents

Urbit Systems Technical Journal I:2 (2024): 105–113.
Address author correspondence to ~palfun-foslup.

1 Improving Eyre HTTP Caching

This proposal for Eyre's HTTP caching mechanism was released by ~palfun-foslup on ~2022.8.15 and revised through ~2022.8.16.

1.1 Introduction

Urbit's primary role is to function as a webserver, but it is not as fast at that operation as it could be. It would be good if Urbit could comfortably serve hundreds or even thousands of pageviews per minute. (Benchmarks for the status quo are left as an exercise to the reader.)

1.2 Approaches to Improving Performance

There are two primary ways in which the scry namespace can be utilized to make Eyre more performant:[1]

1. **Publication cache**: Eyre can track a publication cache with static, known-ahead-of-time responses bound to specific endpoint paths. Eyre would tell the runtime about these known responses, which the runtime would use to serve up responses to GET requests.

2. **Stateless reads**: The runtime, when receiving a GET request, can scry into Eyre to retrieve a response for it. Eyre might scry into agents to further resolve the read. This way, with GET requests handled as pure reads, they could theoretically be served in parallel.

This document focuses on the publication cache. The latter will not deliver performance gains by itself, may actually incur a performance hit in the "scry miss" case, and has unanswered questions around referential transparency. Some prior art can be found in an old draft PR (#4674).

The publication cache also aligns closely with the imagined future of "solid state subscriptions" and the "shrub namespace",

---

[1] Truthfully, there are probably more than two ways, but these specific two have highest relevance in Eyre's recent history.

wherein new or changed data is explicitly published into the namespace.

1.3 Kinds of Content

Before talking about the publication cache proper, we must be aware of what kinds of content may get served through Eyre. We identify three kinds:

1. **Static content** is fully self-contained and only changes when the data within changes; for example: a blog post without comments, or an image.

2. **Dynamic content** changes based on the current state of an agent (or some other datum); for example: a blog post *with* comments or a list of pals.

3. **Procedural content** is generated from the request itself. While the response for any given path may be known ahead of time, it may not be possible to enumerate all the valid paths for which we have responses; for example: a parameterized `/sigil.svg` endpoint, or a calculator API.

Note that for dynamic and procedural content, it may not always be possible to publish a known response at all. If the response depends on the timestamp of the request in some way, a cache entry would be busted before it even got stored. We simply ignore this case.

1.4 Sources of Content

Briefly, take note that for both dynamic and procedural content, Hoon code *must* be executed to generate the (original) response. Most commonly, this takes the form of a Gall userspace agent. In rare cases, generators serve this function.

For static content (only) can we consider another source: Clay, the file system vane. For things that are already files, it makes sense to stick these in Clay. (Think JavaScript blobs, image files, and other "earth" content.) For data that originates within agents, however, in most cases it is unergonomic and unsound to store that data in Clay, especially if the agent may want to refer back to the data later.

In practice, both the "dynamic/prodecural response from agent" and "static file from Clay" cases are common, though the latter is often handled through Docket's "glob" system instead (for, at this point, largely historical reasons).

1.5   Static Publication Cache

Accounting for the fact that agent-driven responses are already common, and weighing the fact that Eyre does not currently have any connection to or dependency on Clay, we propose the following model for a publication cache in Eyre:

```
+$  task
  $%  to-cache
      etc...
  ==
  ::
+$  gift
  $%  to-cache
      etc...
  ==
  ::
+$  to-cache
  $%  [%save endpoint data=simple-payload:http]
      [%dump endpoint]
  ==
  ::
+$  endpoint  ::    exact binding
  $:  binding
      tail=(unit @t)
  ==
```

1. Eyre gets a new task and gift, %save, which can be used to publish responses for a specific endpoint (optional site, plus path, plus extension if any) into the cache.

2. Eyre stores the cache within itself. Whenever something gets added, it notifies the runtime. On-%born, it notifies

the runtime of all existing entries.

3. The runtime tracks the cache as per Eyre's notifications. Whenever it receives a GET request, and an entry for that exact path exists in the cache, it serves the stored response instead of injecting the request as an event.

4. %save may be used to overwrite existing entries. %dump may be used to remove existing entries.

5. When resolving an incoming GET request, Eyre checks the cache for an exact match. If there is, it serves that. If there is none, it falls back to the regular binding matching that path, if any.

This is sufficient to let agents publish responses into the cache, and keep those updated as the underlying data changes.

The "static file from Clay" case can be implemented using the affordances here. To avoid repetition of boilerplate patterns regarding this, we might ship a small piece of userspace infrastructure, an /app/file-server if you will, that is responsible for bindings of this kind.

1.5.1 Authentication

The above does not account for authentication, limiting cached responses to fully public content. Presently, we do not have the affordances needed to handle private content properly.

But it doesn't have to be that way. The %save task could simply include an auth=? flag alongside the data, indicating whether authentication is required or not. The runtime would then, where needed, check the incoming request for a valid authentication cookie, and either give the response or serve a simple 403.

... except that the runtime does not presently know how to check an incoming request for authentication. And making it do so is outside the scope of the grant. The changes here aren't too big though, and in some ways similar to the behavior outlined above. (Most likely, just Eyre telling the runtime about creation/expiry of session identifiers, and teaching the runtime how to check for its presence in any `Cookie` headers.) Considering the very-nice-to-have nature of support for private endpoints, we (read: ~palfun-foslup) may offer to implement this in the short-term, so that the grant work may make use of it.

Caching may not seem as relevant for private content, since it's significantly less likely to get requested many times a minute. But being able to eagerly cache there still provides tangible benefits. Urbit-generated web UIs can get served faster, and private endpoints stop being surface area for DOS attacks.

1.6   Procedural Publication Cache

At this point, we have accounted for serving static and dynamic content from Eyre, but are not yet able to serve procedural content. This requires a slightly different approach.[2]

```
+$  to-cache
  $%  [%prep =binding =work]
      [%drop =binding]
      etc...
  ==

  ::

+$  work  $-(inbound-request simple-payload:http)

  ::

+$  action
  $%  [%work work]
      etc...
  ==
```

1. Eyre gets a new task and gift, `%prep`, which can be used to publish a response generation function for a specific binding (optional site, plus top-level path) into the cache.

2. In addition to a cache entry, Eyre stores this among the normal bindings. Whenever a `%work` binding gets added, Eyre notifies the runtime.

---

[2]The approach outlined in this subsection is still tentative and under discussion, pending solid state subscriptions becoming more "real". Certainly the static publication cache above should be sufficient for most cases.

3. The runtime tracks the cache as per Eyre's notifications. Whenever it receives a `GET` request, it checks to see if a `%prep` binding matches. If one does, it runs the gate and serves the generated response, instead of injecting the request as an event.

4. When resolving an incoming `GET` request, Eyre resolves from the bindings as normal.

However, an important caveat holds at this point in the discussion: how procedural content forces one to bind on non-exact paths, in turn forcing the runtime to bind resolution. We could reduce the friction here by moving Eyre's funtion to find the binding for a given request path into `/sys/lull` or the ivory pill. Alternatively, Eyre just publishes one overarching cache resolution function to the runtime, instead of letting it implement its own logic. Concern with any of these is keeping old copies of the kernel around within these functions. Eyre could re-publish the function(s) on-upgrade, but might also need agents to do the same.

2   Further Thoughts

This document is an alternative proposal by `~rovyns-ricfer` *and* `~master-morzod` *on* `~2022.8.16`. *It particularly emphasizes the role that the bound scry namespace and remote scry play in Urbit's prioritization of referential transparency.*

This represents a vision for how HTTP handling in Urbit could work in the long-run:

1. First check if the URL is immutable, mapped to a fully qualified scry path.

2. Then check if the URL is in a mapping from mutable URL to runtime cache value, which is either:

   (a) an HTTP 307 temporary redirect to a fully qualified scry path, or

   (b) a direct HTTP response value

3. If neither of these, then inject the request into Arvo as an event.

Most read requests should use the namespace rather than directly cached values. This promotes having as much of the system as possible built on referential transparency, which facilitates scaling. However, if a request would be better served without an HTTP redirect (such as a request for a top-level webpage where the URL should not include a revision number or other scry-related details), then an application can ask Eyre to serve the response directly (and the runtime can cache this value, as long as it invalidates it properly when it changes).

If we want Eyre to serve a login page without external dependencies, for example, it should use the mapping from mutable URL to direct value – but if it's fine to put it in Clay, then it can redirect to the namespace.

In the future, we'll want to allow the runtime to handle authentication with minimal Arvo activation. This would prevent unnecessary events being enqueued – which could be used for denial of service attacks – and it also could be used to enable access to private scryable data. A user could authenticate and retrieve a (potentially mutable) piece of scryable data without activating Arvo, or only activating it to validate an authentication token.

Given this context, the mutable mapping we're trying to implement in this PR could be thought of as a subset of the second check here, namely mutable values that map directly to HTTP response values stored in Eyre and cached in the runtime.

Alternatively, we could treat this as the other version of the second check, involving a redirect: Eyre could maintain a referentially transparent mapping from mutable URL to scry path, and the runtime could mirror this mapping and also have a scry cache that it uses to serve HTTP scry requests after the redirects.

There are multiple considerations pointing us toward using direct HTTP responses for now:

1. The ergonomics of Clay:

(a) We need a separate desk full of marks for all served files.

(b) We need mark conversions from all filetypes to HTTP response.

(c) We need to name each desk, with ad-hoc namespacing.

(d) We need to establish tombstoning policies ("norms").

2. Limitations on the namespace for Gall agents:

(a) Only scry at current date.

(b) No solid-state publications yet.

(c) Lack of permissioning.

3. Desire to have full control over the URL shown to a user in a browser.

Given all of these concerns, Eyre development should prioritize implementing direct responses first and the subsequent pieces at a later time.▨

References

~palfun-foslup (~2024..) "urbit/urbit #4674: king: scry on GET requests (WIP)". URL: https://github.com/urbit/urbit/pull/4674 (visited on ~2024.9.11).

A noun is an atom or a cell. An atom is a natural number.
A cell is an ordered pair of nouns.

Reduce by the first matching pattern; variables match any noun.

```
nock(a)                  *a
[a b c]                  [a [b c]]

?[a b]                   0
?a                       1
+[a b]                   +[a b]
+a                       1 + a
=[a a]                   0
=[a b]                   1

/[1 a]                   a
/[2 a b]                 a
/[3 a b]                 b
/[(a + a) b]             /[2 /[a b]]
/[(a + a + 1) b]         /[3 /[a b]]
/a                       /a

#[1 a b]                 a
#[(a + a) b c]           #[a [b /[(a + a + 1) c]] c]
#[(a + a + 1) b c]       #[a [/[(a + a) c] b] c]
#a                       #a

*[a [b c] d]             [*[a b c] *[a d]]

*[a 0 b]                 /[b a]
*[a 1 b]                 b
*[a 2 b c]               *[*[a b] *[a c]]
*[a 3 b]                 ?*[a b]
*[a 4 b]                 +*[a b]
*[a 5 b c]               =[*[a b] *[a c]]

*[a 6 b c d]             *[a *[[c d] 0 *[[2 3] 0 *[a 4 4 b]]]]
*[a 7 b c]               *[*[a b] c]
*[a 8 b c]               *[[*[a b] a] c]
*[a 9 b c]               *[*[a c] 2 [0 1] 0 b]
*[a 10 [b c] d]          #[b *[a c] *[a d]]

*[a 11 [b c] d]          *[[*[a c] *[a d]] 0 3]
*[a 11 b c]              *[a c]

*a                       *a
```